D1570891

Alcoholism

Other Books in the Social Issues Firsthand Series:

Alcoholism

Justin Karr, Book Editor

GREENHAVEN PRESS

An imprint of Thomson Gale, a part of The Thomson Corporation

Detroit • New York • San Francisco • New Haven, Conn. • Waterville, Maine • London

Christine Nasso, *Publisher*
Elizabeth Des Chenes, *Managing Editor*

© 2007 The Gale Group.

Star logo is a trademark and Gale and Greenhaven Press are registered trademarks used herein under license.

For more information, contact:
Greenhaven Press
27500 Drake Rd.
Farmington Hills, MI 48331-3535
Or you can visit our Internet site at http://www.gale.com

LIBRARY OF CONGRESS CATALOGING-IN-PUBLICATION DATA

Alcoholism / Justin Karr, book editor.
    p. cm. -- (Social issues firsthand)
    Includes bibliographical references and index.
    ISBN-13: 978-0-7377-3832-2 (hardcover)
    1. Alcoholism--United States. 2. Teenagers--Alcohol use--United States.
3. Alcoholics--Family relationships--United States. 4. Alcoholics--Rehabil-
itation--United States. I. Karr, Justin.
    HV5292.A38554 2008
    362.292--dc22
                                                                2007024135

ISBN-10: 0-7377-3832-4 (hardcover)

Printed in the United States of America
10 9 8 7 6 5 4 3 2 1

Contents

Chapter 1: Alcohol and Teens

Chapter 2: Coping with a Parent's Addiction

Chapter 3: Alcoholism from the Perspective of Family and Friends

Chapter 4: Recovery

Foreword

Social issues are often viewed in abstract terms. Pressing challenges such as poverty, homelessness, and addiction are viewed as problems to be defined and solved. Politicians, social scientists, and other experts engage in debates about the extent of the problems, their causes, and how best to remedy them. Often overlooked in these discussions is the human dimension of the issue. Behind every policy debate over poverty, homelessness, and substance abuse, for example, are real people struggling to make ends meet, to survive life on the streets, and to overcome addiction to drugs and alcohol. Their stories are ubiquitous and compelling. They are the stories of everyday people—perhaps your own family members or friends—and yet they rarely influence the debates taking place in state capitols, the national Congress, or the courts.

The disparity between the public debate and private experience of social issues is well illustrated by looking at the topic of poverty. Each year the U.S. Census Bureau establishes a poverty threshold. A household with an income below the threshold is defined as poor, while a household with an income above the threshold is considered able to live on a basic subsistence level. For example, in 2003 a family of two was considered poor if its income was less than $12,015; a family of four was defined as poor if its income was less than $18,810. Based on this system, the bureau estimates that 35.9 million Americans (12.5 percent of the population) lived below the poverty line in 2003, including 12.9 million children below the age of eighteen.

Commentators disagree about what these statistics mean. Social activists insist that the huge number of officially poor Americans translates into human suffering. Even many families that have incomes above the threshold, they maintain, are likely to be struggling to get by. Other commentators insist that the statistics exaggerate the problem of poverty in the United States. Compared to people in developing countries, they point out, most so-called poor families have a high quality of life. As stated by journalist Fidelis Iyebote, "Cars are owned by 70 percent of 'poor' households. . . . Color televisions belong to 97 percent of the 'poor' [and] videocassette recorders belong to nearly 75 percent. . . . Sixty-four percent have microwave ovens, half own a stereo system, and over a quarter possess an automatic dishwasher."

However, this debate over the poverty threshold and what it means is likely irrelevant to a person living in poverty. Simply put, poor people do not need the government to tell them whether they are poor. They can see it in the stack of bills they cannot pay. They are aware of it when they are forced to choose between paying rent or buying food for their children. They become painfully conscious of it when they lose their homes and are forced to live in their cars or on the streets. Indeed, the written stories of poor people define the meaning of poverty more vividly than a government bureaucracy could ever hope to. Narratives composed by the poor describe losing jobs due to injury or mental illness, depict horrific tales of childhood abuse and spousal violence, recount the loss of friends and family members. They evoke the slipping away of social supports and government assistance, the descent into substance abuse and addiction, the harsh realities of life on the streets. These are the perspectives on poverty that are too often omitted from discussions over the extent of the problem and how to solve it.

Greenhaven Press's Social Issues Firsthand series provides a forum for the often-overlooked human perspectives on society's most divisive topics of debate. Each volume focuses on one social issue and presents a collection of ten to sixteen narratives by those who have had personal involvement with the topic. Extra care has been taken to include a diverse range of perspectives. For example, in the volume on adoption, readers will find the stories of birth parents who have made an adoption plan, adoptive parents, and adoptees themselves. After exposure to these varied points of view, the reader will have a clearer understanding that adoption is an intense, emotional experience full of joyous highs and painful lows for all concerned.

The debate surrounding embryonic stem cell research illustrates the moral and ethical pressure that the public brings to bear on the scientific community. However, while nonexperts often criticize scientists for not considering the potential negative impact of their work, ironically the public's reaction against such discoveries can produce harmful results as well. For example, although the outcry against embryonic stem cell research in the United States has resulted in fewer embryos being destroyed, those with Parkinson's, such as actor Michael J. Fox, have argued that prohibiting the development of new stem cell lines ultimately will prevent a timely cure for the disease that is killing Fox and thousands of others.

Each book in the series contains several features that enhance its usefulness, including an in-depth introduction, an annotated table of contents, bibliographies for further research, a list of organizations to contact, and a thorough index. These elements—combined with the poignant voices of people touched by tragedy and triumph—make the Social Issues Firsthand series a valuable resource for research on today's topics of political discussion.

Introduction

Although alcohol purchase and consumption are illegal throughout the United States for those under the age of twenty-one, alcohol continues to be the most widely abused substance for middle school and high school students. In 2005, rates of alcohol use for twelve- and thirteen-year-olds stood at 4.2 percent. For fourteen- and fifteen-year-olds the number rose to 15.1 percent and for sixteen- and seventeen-year-olds it was 30.1 percent. An astounding 51.1 percent of young people ages eighteen to twenty were using alcohol.[1] Many of these adolescents may be classified as alcoholics, or those suffering from alcohol addiction. Teenage alcoholism affects all races, economic levels, and geographic areas.

Teenage Drinking and Alcoholism

Alcoholism is defined as "the consumption of or preoccupation with alcoholic beverages to the extent that this behavior interferes with the alcoholic's normal personal, family, social, or work life."[2] Alcohol can be both physically and psychologically addictive. It impacts the body by depressing the central nervous system—leading to slowed reactions, slurred speech, and ultimately to vomiting, unconsciousness, and even death. Alcohol use by young people is especially dangerous because of the emotional immaturity of most teenagers. According to research by the National Center on Addiction and Substance Abuse, "Individuals who begin drinking before the age of 15 are four times more likely to become alcohol dependent than those who begin drinking at age 21."[3]

Most teenagers begin by "binge drinking" at parties or other social events with their peers. Binge drinking is generally understood as the consumption of five or more drinks in a row by males or four or more drinks in a row by females. A study of high school seniors has revealed that 80 percent report binge drinking, getting drunk, or drinking and driving, and of those students, over 50 percent admitted that drinking had made them feel ill, get arrested, have a car accident, and miss school or work.[4]

With the knowledge that alcohol use is not only illegal for minors, but also causes numerous problems, why would so many young people continue to take the risk to drink alcohol? Most teens admit that they begin drinking alcohol due to peer pressure or the desire to "fit in." They enjoy the "liquid courage" that alcohol gives them in social situations and the escape from their personal problems, including mental illness and family conflict, that drinking seems to provide. As recovering alcoholic Lisa remembers, "When I was 14 my best friend and I went to a party and we got drunk for the first time. We both vomited and got into big trouble. But far from putting me off, the experience gave me a confidence that I never felt when I was sober. I had a positive association with drinking right from the start. I suddenly thought I was funny and witty. I thought I was more attractive. I began to believe that I needed to drink to have those conversations."[5]

The belief that alcohol is a cure-all for adolescent woes is encouraged by alcohol companies, as well as the media and Hollywood. In 2002, alcohol companies in the United States spent $1.9 billion on magazine, newspaper, television, radio, and outdoor advertisements for their products.[6] These ads tend to glamorize alcohol consumption, linking it with confidence, enjoyment, and sex appeal. In response to increases in adolescent exposure to alcohol advertising in magazines, public health scholar Ralph Hingson of Boston University wondered, "Are these advertising and promotional practices contributing to the declining age of alcohol use initiation, which in turn increases the risk of alcohol dependence and other alcohol problems affecting drinkers and people with whom they come in contact both during adolescence and adulthood?"[7] In addition to alcohol-related advertisements, teens are exposed to underage drinking through celebrity lifestyle choices and media coverage. Recently, for example, many teenage celebrities have admitted to being alcoholics and have entered into rehabilitation programs before even reaching the legal age to purchase and consume alcohol. The partying lifestyle of such celebrities takes center stage in the media rather than the devastation caused to their personal lives and careers due to alcohol abuse.

Sobriety and Hope for the Teenage Alcoholic

While it may seem that all teens drink alcohol, many teenagers are outspokenly against alcohol abuse and join groups such as SADD (Students Against Destructive Decisions). SADD encourages youth to have fun, enjoy life, and nurture positive personal relationships without drinking. Others simply set a positive example for their peers by choosing to abstain from alcohol. As author Tynan explained on his popular blog BetterThanYourBoyfriend.com, "I don't need or want the things [alcohol] offers. I'm already secure, inhibition-free, happy, unstressed, and have enough great friends to prevent me from being lonely or bored. What could I possibly gain?"[8] Lauren, a new college student, has realized, "It may seem like a lot of fun at parties, but the after effects are not worth it. . . . One thing that's aided me [in avoiding alcohol] is to find a group of friends that don't want to drink. If you have someone to do something with on the weekends, you won't feel obligated to attend parties that have alcohol. Rent some fun movies, make a fancy dinner, go to a local museum; . . . there are plenty of options that do not involve drinking that are equally fun."[9]

If a teenager does develop a drinking problem, help is readily available. One of the most popular support services for addicts is Alcoholics Anonymous (AA). AA is an international support group; its only requirement for membership is a desire to stop drinking. Many chapters of AA hold meetings specifically for young people. Alternatively, teens concerned about alcoholism among their friends or family members may seek support through Alateen. Together, the members of this organization share their experiences, discuss their difficulties, examine their relationships with alcoholics, and learn effective ways to cope with their problems without relying on alcohol.

Social Issues Firsthand: Alcoholism addresses the topic of alcohol and teens, presenting the stories of adolescents who have coped with either their own or a loved one's alcoholism. It provides first-hand accounts of alcoholics who have experienced personal growth through recovery and includes viewpoints from the friends and family of addicts. As Joseph A. Califano Jr. of the National Center on Addiction and Substance Abuse at Columbia University has said, "A child who reaches age 21 without smoking, abusing alcohol or using drugs is virtually certain never to do so."[10] While the short-term enjoyment derived from alcohol use may seem desirable to many young people, the long-term consequences are often devastating. There is hope for teens who develop an addiction, but the most successful way to avoid alcoholism is to choose not to drink in the first place.

Notes

1. "Teenage Alcohol Use Statistics," AlcoholismResources.com, www.alcoholismresources.com/teenage_alcoholism_statistics.html.
2. "Alcoholism," Wikipedia, the free encyclopedia, www.en.wikipedia.org/wiki/Alcoholism.
3. "Press Releases 2002: CASA Report on Underage Drinking," The National Center on Addiction and Substance Abuse at Columbia University, February 26, 2002, http://www.casacolumbia.org/absolutenm/templates/PressReleases.aspx?articleid=271&zoneid=47.
4. "Teenage Drinking," www.teenage-drinking.net.
5. Deborah Herd, "A Shot in the Dark," *Shape* magazine Web site, http://www.shapemag.co.za/article.php?id=418.
6. "Underage Girls More Exposed to Alcohol Ads than Boys or Adults in USA," *Medical News Today*, July 6, 2004, http://www.medicalnewstoday.com/medicalnews.php?newsid=10345.
7. Ibid
8. "Why I Don't Drink," Better Than Your Boyfriend blog, May 16, 2006, http://www.betterthanyourboyfriend.com/206.htm.

9. "Alcohol: From the Mentors," PBS Kids website, http://pbskids.org/itsmylife/body/alcohol/mentors.html.

10. "Alcohol and Teen Drinking," Focus Adolescent Services website, http://www.focusas.com/Alcohol.html.

SOCIAL ISSUES
FIRSTHAND

CHAPTER 1

Alcohol and Teens

A Near-Death Experience from Alcohol

Koren Zailckas

In the following excerpt from Koren Zailckas's Smashed: Story of a Drunken Girlhood, *the author details her first blackout from alcohol at the age of sixteen. Zailckas was at a party drinking with friends when she passed out. She was taken to the hospital where her blood alcohol content was registered at 0.25. Zailckas describes the punishment she received from her parents and the estrangement and alienation she felt from her friends after the incident. Zailckas's first book,* Smashed: Story of a Drunken Girlhood, *was a* New York Times *bestseller and was selected by Barnes and Noble for its 2005 Discover Great New Writers program. Zailckas grew up in suburban Boston and attended Syracuse University. She lives in New York City.*

Henceforth, my mother will refer to it as the time I almost died. We'll be sitting in the kitchen, both four and seven years from now. My dad will extend the leaves of the kitchen table to accommodate whatever college boyfriend I've brought home for the weekend. And my mom, while spooning out three-bean salad, will turn and ask him, "Has Koren told you about the time she almost died?"

I'll never know how much of that assertion accounts for melodrama.

Sure enough, it feels like death. On November 9, 1996, I wake up between the Tide-stiff sheets of my childhood Banister Bed and one thought occurs to me: *I'm not wearing any underwear.*

Unable to Remember

This is all the information I need to know that something horrendous has happened. At sixteen, I am never naked, save for ten minutes a day under the stream of a morning shower, and even then, I turn away from the bathroom mirror before I drop my towel to step in. Even alone, I am ashamed of the arcs of my own pale skin, particularly in the whitest part that spans between my hips. Given my tendency to thrash in my sleep and kick down sheets, I would never sleep without underwear.

My bed looks like it's been made with me in it. There's not a wrinkle in the comforter; its patched pastel pattern is pulled smooth and tight, clear up to my neck. When I start to unroll my arms and legs from the folds of the sheets, I feel a sharp pain in my elbow, like I've been sleeping on it, and I stop for a moment, trying to decide if that position is physically possible.

I decide to fold back the comforter from one corner, the way someone might diagonally halve a dinner napkin. I do it slowly. It's like opening a hand-addressed letter with no return address; I have a feeling I could find just about anything inside.

What I find under the covers looks like someone else's nightgown. It is a thin, white, cotton smock, stippled with green, and it cuts off at my knees. I can't imagine who I borrowed it from, since my friends and I all sleep in nylon shorts and our dads' XL T-shirts. When I feel around to the breach of cloth above my own pink ass, it dawns on me: *I'm wearing a hospital gown.*

I'm immobile in the face of my panic. I'm stunned to the point that I don't dare breathe or kick my feet in a way that would make even the faintest sliding sound on the starched sheets. I don't know how many minutes I lay like this, motionless in the small sag that my body makes in the mattress, barely breathing. I can't get out of bed until I've figured out what emergency landed me in this green and white gown. My room is directly above the dining room, and the littlest thump on the carpet can shake the chandelier; I don't want anyone downstairs to see it swinging and know I'm awake.

I feel like I'm arriving at the scene of an accident, like my physical self has been creamed in a hit-and-run and my mental self is the first one to find it. All I can do is run through the basic first-aid checkpoints, the first of which is: *Can you move?*

I pull my knees into my chest and wrap both arms around them with no problem, aside from the throbbing deep in my elbow. The back of my head is tender against the pillow, and my neck moves in a succession of arthritic-like cracks. But my joints move. I'm not paralyzed.

There are no clues in the form of a cast or a bandage or stitches. Lying down, I can't even make out any discernible bruises. Later, I'll be able to make out the purple impressions of fingers around my biceps, plus a golf ball-sized bruise on one ass cheek, a sort of yellowed half-moon around a raised, blue bump. But for now, the only visible signs that I'm injured are the hospital gown and a pink, plastic wristband that reads ZAILCKAS, KOREN.

The house is filled with the sounds of Saturday morning in motion. Bear is barking to be let in through the side door. There is the sound of coffee mugs clinking on countertops, and I detect the faint smell of bagels burning in the oven. I might even hear the far-off sound of my mother's whirring laughter.

My room appears equal in its sameness. There are dirty socks on the floor and stacks of *Seventeen* on my desk. On my bureau, there are notebooks on top of snapshots, necklaces on top of notebooks, and dust over just about everything, ever since I barred my mom from my room. Fall light filters through the window blinds and casts sunny stripes across the carpet. I can see my back-to-school sweaters brushing elbows in the closet; the price tags are still stapled to some of them, and I can make out the orange half-off stickers from Filene's juniors' department.

The Night Before

Mentally, I retrace my steps from last night to try to find this dropped memory.

As far as Friday nights go, it was typical. I spent it with my new friend, Kat Caldwell. She is a girl I made friends with a few months ago for no real reason other than we both drink and we're both sensitive. The first night I'd slept over at Kat's house, I saw that her sheets were streaked with mascara, and her Laura Ashley pillowcases retained the outline of her whole face: half-moon of foundation, faint ring of lip stain, black strokes from the flurried beating of her dripping eyelashes. She'd opened the drawers of her bureau to show me the old liquor bottles she hid under her childhood ballet costumes, and I'd laughed at dozens of tiny Lycra bodices, net tutus, and loose sequins that smelled of Tanqueray.

Kat came with a silver cord to more friends, like Abby and Allen, and I'd gone with all of them, plus my childhood friend Claire, to a Friday-night get-together near the lake in the next town over.

A girl whose parents were away in Vermont for a wine-tasting weekend threw the party. Her parents must have warned her not to have friends over while they were gone because she wouldn't let any of us inside her house to mix drinks properly, in cups. Instead, about a dozen of us—friends, and friends of friends, and neighborhood kids who'd heard that someone's parents were out—were in the backyard, slugging rum, tequila, and Kahlúa straight from their bottles. At one point, when I asked the girl if I could go inside to use her bathroom, she suggested that I drop my pants behind the hedges across the street.

The whole ordeal hadn't been the least bit thrilling. I'd sat beside Kat on a splintering dock. Our bare feet dangled over the edge of the black, rippling water, where we could occasionally hear fish jump, making plopping sounds like tossed coins. The wind propelled dead leaves across the lake's surface. The clouds swirled themselves around the moon.

I started by taking small sips from the communal bottles. I knocked back a few sips of generic rum, which tasted strong and acidic, and bit my throat. I soothed it with candied gulps of Kahlúa.

I also drank from a thermos filled with vodka that Claire had filched from a bottle in her parents' liquor cabinet. It was the same gallon-wide jug of Absolut that we always stole from, and then added water to, in an effort to recover the stolen inches. After months of adding and subtracting, the vodka had reached a diluted state that rendered it tasteless. It was as cold and wet as springwater, and we drank it fast.

The last thing I remember is telling Claire about the poet Frank O'Hara, the way he'd said that "after the first glass of vodka you can accept anything about life, even your own mysteriousness. After that, my own mystery opens up."

Wearing a Hospital Gown

There are only so many calamities that could have warranted this hospital gown. My first thought is that I lost my footing on the path leading up from the dock and cracked my knee in the place where it still wasn't fully healed from the surgery. One would think I'd remember that kind of fall, but perhaps the pain of it blacked me out.

For one horrible moment, it also occurs to me that Allen, who had driven, might have had too many sips of straight rum and veered the car off the road on the way home. It was only a month ago that a boy in our class got drunk and drove his car into a lake, where it sunk like an old tire, and he had to unroll the window to swim out. For a moment, I think whiplash could be responsible for my lumped head and stiff neck, not to mention the amnesia. But then I decide I'd surely remember something from the moments before we crashed: gasping, blackness spreading across the windshield, the sound of pine branches scraping the flanks of the car.

I should call one of the girls who'd been with me, to see if they can fill in the gaps. But when I look for the portable phone, someone has removed it from its cradle on my bureau, as if to prevent that from happening.

I step softly to my full-length mirror, using the ballet-walk where you stand only on the balls of your feet.

The image reflected back at me makes me cup my mouth with both hands: I look like a woman in a zombie film from the 1950s. My hair looks like it's been replaced with a Halloween wig; it is teased into a high pile of knots and dusted with dirt and leaves, and something sticky has lacquered the ends together. From this position, I can make out a whole range of fingerprints that wrap around my forearms in shades of brownish-blue and yellow. A cat-scratch is carved into the corner of my eye; aside from that, my face looks slack and pasty, but unmarked.

I can see now that I'm wearing hospital booties with my gown. They are blue ankle-socks with plastic beads on the soles, presumably so you won't slip on the linoleum floors while you're fleeing the ward.

I add another item to the list of possible accidents: psychiatric emergency.

My alarm clock says it's 10:30. That tells me that whatever happened must be serious because no one has bothered to wake me for my poetry workshop. I was scheduled to spend the weekend at a conference for Worcester County's most promising young writers, and it started more than two hours ago. The workshop is one of those college résumé padders that my mother would send me to in any state short of death. (Just two months ago, she *forced* me to spend a week at diplomacy camp at Washington, D.C., and just to spite her, I'd skipped the lectures on youth leadership to buy forties of beer and drink them with local delinquents on the hill behind the dorm.)

I would stay in my room all day, trying to figure out what happened, if I didn't desperately need a glass of water. My throat is so parched it feels raw, and each swallow is arduous.

I keep the hospital booties on because the morning has the cold nip of fall, but I trade the gown for a sweatshirt and a pair of flannel pants. I try to brush my hair, and realize with one painful stroke that the task could take all afternoon, so instead I wind the whole snarled mess into a lopsided bun. I look at myself in the mirror and wince before heading downstairs to meet my parents with the premonition that I am fucked.

The Blackout

It is my first blackout.

I will never again experience one so comprehensive. I get the details first from Claire, who I find pretending to sleep on the couch in the living room. My parents will rehash them with me again later, as will Kat and Allen and Abby when I see them Monday morning at school. The remaining gaps I'll fill in years later, when I get the courage to ask my father more questions, and when I see my emergency file.

I passed out on the dock in a puddle of my own vomit. I imagine it was mostly liquor because my dad told the doctor I didn't eat dinner that night. Before that, I pulled my shirt up over my shoulders to show my bra to someone's brother because, knowing I was slipping into oblivion, he'd asked me what color it was. I'd also professed a soul-shattering love for an older boy who had taken me for a drunken walk in the woods a few months earlier—a boy who had pushed my back into the cragged banks of a stream and called me a baby when I wouldn't let him pull off my underwear.

After I tottered and fell sideways onto the planks of the dock, nobody could wake me. Allen, Abby, Claire, and Kat carried me up the hill to the road by my arms and legs, which is why my body bears what look like forty finger-shaped bruises. They dropped me a few times, too, which explains the raised bumps on my butt and the back of my head.

When they tell me this, I envision a dead body—not my body, but the body of someone in a thriller movie who has just been clubbed with a paperweight and dragged in a bloody streak across the floor by her feet. When I ask them why they didn't roll me up in a rug, no one finds it funny.

The girl whose house we were at brought out a pair of pilled sweatpants because I'd retched all over my jeans. I can't imagine that she would have let me inside, given that I was liable to puke over all manner of Venetian rugs and calico curtains, so I'll come to imagine that they pulled off my jeans outside on the porch, leaving my underwear fully exposed while they struggled to stick my feet through the sweatpants' elasticized legs. Then they draped me across the backseat of Allen's car and drove me to Abby's house.

From what I can tell from the medical records, this whole ordeal took at least an hour. It was around 12:30. Abby's parents were asleep when my friends lugged me in through the front door.

They tried to give me a shower, to clean off the combination of liquor, vomit, dirt, and leaves that was adhered to me. I'll never know if I was fully naked or if they left my underthings on because I am too embarrassed to ask. Nor will I know if Allen was there while they did it, though I don't know how they could have held me under the showerhead without his strength. Afterward, they must have put me back into the sweatpants because they are there in the plastic bag that my dad carried home from the hospital, and they are all but crusted with vomit. My mom will wash them and insist that I return them, in a most undignified moment, to the girl at school on Monday morning.

By the time I was showered, I had already missed my curfew, so Abby called my father to tell him not to worry. She said I'd fallen asleep while we were watching a movie and asked if I could stay the night.

My father hadn't believed her. He asked to speak to her parents, and when she said they were sleeping, he asked to talk to me. I was dangling over the edge of her brother's bunk bed, getting sick again. In a second-long flash of memory, I recall someone shaking my shoulders and telling me to pull it together for two minutes, probably so I could ask my dad if I could stay the night. When they held the receiver to my ear, I slurred, "I'll be home in fifteen minutes, Daddy."

Years later, he will say it was one of those pivotal moments—he sensed that the whole world swung on whether he went back to sleep or drove to me.

In the Emergency Room

Claire went to the hospital with my father. She was an emergency medical trainee and knew how to calculate heart rates and breaths per minute, which she did throughout the thirty-minute drive.

After everything, it is the thought of Claire answering my dad's questions that makes me feel most guilty. He is intimidating when he's not trying to be, and bloodcurdling when he is. If he puts the full boom into his voice, he can make boyfriends tremble and customer-service reps cry. When he asked Claire what happened, she told him nearly the whole truth. She injected fiction only when he asked where we got the vodka—she said older boys from the neighborhood brought it, instead of admitting that we poured it from her parents' depository of Absolut jugs.

When the car pulled up in front of the emergency room, my father says, he carried me through the doors the way he used to carry me to bed.

The doctors tested my urine for drugs. According to the doctor's notes, it was the only time I showed signs of life. When the nurse was trying to insert a catheter I kept muttering, "Stop, it's embarrassing," proving that even semiconscious, I was self-conscious. In my chart, there are ten pages of lab results, including all sorts of decimal numbers and strands of letters that I don't understand, but really don't need to. Alcohol alone was responsible for knocking me out, a combination of rum and vodka and coffee liqueur. On one page there is a long list of chemical compounds for which I came up NONDETECT.

Claire tells me the doctors seemed certain they would find some substance, besides alcohol, sweeping through my system. It is the year that everyone first read about Rohypnol, the brand name for flunitrazepam, the tranquilizer used to treat sleeplessness, anxiety, convulsions, and muscle tension. Four months earlier, two women who had been raped after someone slipped them Rohypnol testified before Congress to urge them to take action against the vast numbers of people who were smuggling the drug into the United States. One of them said of the man who raped her, "This guy could have sawed me in half and I wouldn't have known the difference." A classification known as "date-rape drugs" had emerged. And everyone in the ER thought I was on them.

My dad will say later that the doctors were far less compassionate when my test results revealed I was just another teenaged girl who'd nearly poisoned herself by drinking. I will always wonder, though, if the staff's lack of sympathy had more to do with another brief flash of a memory, in which I clawed at the tubes tethered to my arm and screamed at the faint impression of a woman, maybe a doctor or nurse, calling her a "dumb-ass bitch."

Alcohol Poisoning

No one could imagine that I'd done this to myself. My dad, particularly, was convinced that someone held a gun to my head. It was beyond his comprehension that I'd willed myself to this level of past gone. I was an A student in English, psychology, and art. Sure, math and science were touch-and-go, but that just meant I was right-brained. As far as he knew, will was what I reserved for the PSATs and ballet auditions. It was what I used to solicit cash for the mall.

My charts say my skin was cold and clammy, which is one of the signs of alcohol poisoning, as is the fact that I was only semi-conscious. When my tests came back they showed my blood alcohol content to be 0.25. A 0.4 BAC is considered lethal for the average person, but it can take less for young people and first-time drinkers.

At sixteen, I'm 5'2" and 105 pounds with a ski parka on, which means it would take about one hour of downing eight to ten drinks to kill me. Claire told the doctors I'd been drinking for an hour and a half. I'd had half a thermos of vodka, plus immeasurable sips of rum and Kahlúa, straight from the bottles. As the doctor told my father, a few more drinks and I'd have fell into a coma or died right there on the dock.

No matter how many ways I go over the story, I'll never know if some part of me sought that kind of close call. A good bit of it was inexperience; it was not waiting for all those gulps of liquor to absorb into my system, but just expecting to feel them right away. But I also wonder if that night wasn't the first glimmer of a budding death drive, what Freud called the instinct we all have to return to the perfect stillness we felt before birth. Other girls my age steered into that urge with starvation diets or razor blades, but I chose alcohol because it seemed far less fanatical. On nights when I felt sad, particularly, I could feel my drinking accelerate.

I'd been saddened a lot lately, and stressed. Even with new friends like Kat, high school was a nightmarish system of checks and balances. It required observing yourself constantly, making sure you distinguished yourself enough to be accepted, but not to the point where you might garner resentment.

Schoolwork required inscribing index cards for hours, all the while maintaining the illusion that you didn't give a shit about the decimals of your GPA. Getting a date required acting just disinterested enough to make a boy interested in asking you. Every consideration required reconsideration. I'd begun waking up at 4:30 A.M. so I could reappraise my outfit for the school day; the fate of the next two years seemed to weigh on whether I chose suede cowboy boots or Adidas sneakers.

My parents always swore that in my childhood they had to let me win at board games. If, by the lucky stroke of the plastic wheel, my father would accidentally beat me at Candy Land, I would fly into fits of bawling that I'm told would last for hours. If I couldn't triumph, I didn't want to play. I would pack up my toys and go home. This was perhaps how I felt about being sixteen.

But I'll never know if I intended to forfeit. They pumped my stomach, and I sprung back to life that morning in my bedroom. I went directly back to homeroom. I did not pass "Go." I did not collect $200.

Facing the Parents

Saturday, at breakfast, my parents seem almost serene. The coffee is still steaming. The Saturday *Boston Globe* is still spread out beneath us, in sections. My dad is sitting across from me, with his elbows folded on the woven tablecloth my parents bought in Greece early in their marriage. My mom is at the head of the table, with her hands crossed on the paper's business section. Bear is pacing the floor by our feet, hoping for a dropped cube of cantaloupe. The seating arrangement makes me feel like a fox in an English hunting painting. It feels like everyone is closing in around me, and I feel the terror of being surrounded.

My mother starts the conversation and I end up turning sideways in my chair to face her. From this position, I can avoid the gaze of my father, which is sterner on account of his being at the hospital. My mom doesn't try to recap the time line. Instead, she says, "I assume Claire filled you in."

It makes me wonder if my parents had had Claire sleep on the living-room couch because it spared them the awkwardness of rehashing the gory details for me. In fact, we'd waited to have this discussion until my dad and I had driven Claire home. Even with the babble of NPR, the car was so silent I could hear the engine purring.

My mom says the problem is not that I've been experimenting with alcohol; she'd made it clear in Ocean City that I am old enough to do that. In fact, she says, it is probably a good idea for me to toy around with drinking now, while I still live at home, instead of waiting until I get to college, where the environment makes inexperience even more risky.

She says she wouldn't have cared if I'd been drinking at home last night. I could have drunk myself into a similar stupor, she says, gone upstairs, and passed out in my bed. At home, she would have known I was safe. But anything could have happened to me on that dock. She says, "What if you fell into the water and drowned? What if you had been raped?"

My dad says hardly anything. He sets his reading glasses down on top of the front page and looks at me with eyes I don't know how to interpret. I can't remember the last time he looked at me this unremittingly. The moments we spend together usually revolve around some type of project. Typically, we talk while we cook, spray-paint patio furniture, or make candles out of melted-down crayons. Those times, his eyes are focused on the peppers in the wok, or the jet from the paint can, or the bottle we fill with hot wax. He is the type of dad who expresses concern by constructing things, or cooking, or shopping for gadgets, by making sure I have a full stomach, a computer Zip drive, and Gore-Tex boots come spring thaw. I've never seen the expression he is giving me now. It's not outrage, really, or disappointment. It is the look of crude disbelief.

The only concern he voices aloud is about my missing the young writers' conference. He asks (rhetorically, of course), "Do you see how drinking makes you miss out on other fun activities?"

My mother cries a little, which always makes me cry, too. I've always been like a dog in the way that I absorb her moods. I have been listening to my parents speak with a tension like a rock in my throat. As my mother cries, I have to keep swallowing In the end, I give up and bawl soundlessly. I use the sleeve of my sweatshirt to wipe the wetness from my face.

At the time, I think my mother cries solely because I've frightened her. But years from now, more drunken sons and daughters will surface among her relatives and friends. There will be comatose daughters on respirators, daughters laid up in hospitals with broken cheekbones, car accidents, DUI [driving under the influence] charges, and sons whose early admissions to Ivy League universities are threatened by alcohol-related suspensions. Years from now, my mother will explain more to me. She'll say, "When you choose to stay at home to rear your kids, a dead-drunk daughter makes you question an entire decade's worth of motherhood—you wonder if the career you gave up made the slightest difference in the personalities you've been shaping."

My sister is eleven. As luck would have it, she is spending the night at a friend's house, so she misses all the clues that point to this black crime. My mom won't tell her about it until she's eighteen, when it's used as a cautionary tale to warn her off drinking, and by that time the handles of the liquor cabinet will wear a silver luggage lock. My sister will be appalled. But mostly, she'll mourn the fact that, as the youngest, she's always the last to know.

There is not much to say in my defense. There is no point in telling a fraction of the truth because there is no gray area in which to weasel. All the facts of the night are laid out on the table, like plates of fruit and toast.

While my parents talk, I nod like a dashboard Chihuahua and say, "I know, I know, I know." I certainly say I am sorry; it's the only thing I can think to say with the hospital bracelet still sliding up and down my wrist.

I am hangover-free due to the large bags of saline pumped through my forearm's thin veins. Still, I climb the stairs back up to my room and sleep for the rest of the day. It's like slipping back into the hole of the blackout—in sleep, I can forget again.

Tomorrow, I'll go for the second day of the young writers' conference, telling the tweed-jacketed director only that I've been sick. In a low-lit corner classroom, I'll try to write a poem I decide to call "Lush," but I won't be able to come up with more than a few first words, scarred by cross-outs.

I know the whole ordeal needs to be written about. But two days afterward, I am still far too close to the night to see it clearly. I am looking only at the incident, and the result is a lot like the pictures in our biology textbook, taken at microscopic range, the ones that look like billowing clouds until you read the caption and realize you are looking at magnified cotton swabs. Years will pass before I can see the night of my stomach-pumping to scale. I will need the perspective of six more years before I understand what I am looking at.

Punishment

My parents ground me for the remainder of November, which is the cruelest season to be in lockdown. There are school-sponsored carnivals. There are semiformal gymnasium dances. There are evening football games, where mist levitates in the stadium lights. And there are remote keg parties afterward.

There are parties that require a two-mile hike through the thick New England woods, crunching through dead leaves, and dodging the occasional small-town cop on the prowl. There are parties like I'll never know again. The air in the clearing smells of apple orchards, Bud Light, and pine-dense bonfire smoke. The weather seems always on the verge of snow, and some boy, who is sitting on a log a few feet away, always seems to be on the verge of crossing the fire flicker to put his arm around me.

Sometime during my punishment, the guilt I feel as a result of the incident melts away. After a few days, my parents stop talking about the reason I am grounded; they reference it only with raised eyebrows when I make some complaint. Likewise, the girls in the cafeteria, who in those first few days after the accident were a flurry of whispering, direct their attention to somebody else. The alarm I felt that morning in my bedroom fades from memory. It is replaced by the agitation that comes with being restricted.

My parents have never made good wardens, and the Zailckas Home Penitentiary is notoriously low-security. Here, a prisoner is free to leaf through fashion magazines, drive to the video store, or surf Internet chat rooms 'til dawn. Phone calls are unlimited. And time off for good behavior will certainly be afforded, if such a thing ever occurs.

In fact, the only real rule in the house of correction is that I can't leave it. At least, not after prime time. This means bonfire parties are out. So is the repertoire of fictions that I regularly use to disguise them: dinner at Applebee's, movies at the General Cinema, fishing in Harvard, canoeing in Concord, hiking Mount Wachusett, throwing spares at the Bowl-A-Way.

At ten every night, my dad punches the keypad on the security system in a series of calculated beeps, to which a robotic woman's voice answers "Al-arm Sys-tem is on!" I listen to him ascend the stairs to go to bed, to Bear's dog tags jingling two or three steps behind him, and know there is no escape. The entire house stirs whenever the system announces "Al-arm Sys-tem is off!" It's enough to wonder whether it's in place to keep criminals out, or to keep me in.

These nights, the house must look picture-perfect. For a month, my parents never have to answer the question: "It's ten

P.M., do you know where your children are?" My sister and I are sachets stuffed into the pockets of our beds.

Nights, the floodlights from the perennial garden splash light over our front door, where my mother has hung a grapevine wreath. Even with the blinds closed, the light gets tossed against my bedroom wall, too. It's bright enough to read by, and well suited for shadow puppets. I've long forgotten how to lace my fingers into the shape of a barking dog, and opt instead for my favorite gesture, the flipped bird. I examine the silhouette of my middle finger from every imaginable angle, saying "F— you" to no one in particular. I perfect all the various forms—thumb in, thumb out, with a wrist twirl—before I lie down to close my eyes, deciding that I hate just about everyone.

Our house is close enough to the high school that I can hear the noise from its football stadium. There's the low echo of my English teacher's voice, announcing the players' names; the horns from the marching band; the swell of applause after each touchdown; and the bleacher-stomping, which sounds like thunder. Somewhere past the edge of the driveway, the mailbox, the old tire swing, I can hear football season. My friends are sneaking Jack Daniel's in the school parking lot during half-time. There is a play in motion.

The days scuttle by, and I keep myself occupied. I divide my closet into a stack of sweaters to keep, and dresses to bag up for Goodwill. I play GameBoy, drop balls of cookie dough onto aluminum sheets, and watch reruns of *The Real World: Miami*, which is the equivalent of a frontal lobotomy. I go to my math tutor nightly and try to twig the cosine rule for hyperbolic triangles.

I never find the file in the birthday cake, that secret escape through the doggy door or out the guest-room window. I never slither breathless through my father's tomato plants, like Tim Robbins in *The Shawshank Redemption*, to emerge at the neighbors' swing set, rain-soaked, jovial, free! I never give my parents the opportunity to search every doghouse, whore-house, or crackhouse. I pay my debt to society because I'm guilty.

I feel confident I could escape if I wanted to; I could shoulder out a bathroom window and walk the two miles it would take to meet so-and-so at such-and-such a party. The most high-tech safeguards are no match for the sixteen-year-old mind.

But in the end, it is my friends themselves who have the authority to keep me at home. My trip to the hospital doesn't exactly cause our falling-out; we still meet at each other's lockers between classes. In study hall, we still paint our fingernails with a black Magic Marker. They still call me on Saturday afternoons to disclose the details of their Friday nights, filling me in on the party that took place in an abandoned barn or someone's unfinished basement. I am always alerted to who threw up, who was felt up, and how long it took the police chief to show up. But no one is willing to aid and abet my escape. Never comes that call to throw down thy hair.

Fall-Out with Friends

I don't blame them. The only A I was ever afforded in biology was in the chapter on evolution. The idea of the able-bodied predator was the only concept that made sense to me. In nature, everyone roots for the marauder. That's why we'll glue ourselves to Animal Planet for hours, stoned or straight, to watch a pair of African lions descend on a gazelle as though we aren't sure how it will end. Everyone would rather be a lion. If we feel sorry for the lesser species it is only because they were sorry enough to get caught.

That night at the dock, I proved I was the weedy one. And because I couldn't handle my liquor, because that weakness endangered everyone else's drinking with the threat of getting caught, I was temporarily cast aside.

I'd managed to get Abby in trouble. Her parents had stumbled to the door when my dad turned up at her house. Since she hadn't been drunk herself, they only grounded her for a weekend, but it was enough to make Allen and Kat temporarily turn on me. They made me apologize to Abby that Monday during lunch period, and I did, because I felt sorry at the time.

But the more I think about Abby during my house arrest, the less apologetic I feel. I can't be sorry for her or her parents, who ban me from their house afterward on the basis that I'm bad company. I decide her parents are either the world's heaviest sleepers, or they've known the score all along. They've slept through infinite Saturday nights where we mixed drinks in their kitchen, or smoked a joint in their backyard, or passed out dead-drunk in their basement in a group of twenty, looking like victims of a cult mass suicide. I think they look the other way and justify it to themselves by saying that as long as Abby drinks in their house, she is under their control.

A month later, Allen will carry Kat, dead-drunk, into Abby's parents' New Year's Eve dinner party. And as much as I'll be able to empathize, the irony will be almost poetic. After it happens, I'll think her parents will retract their harsh judgment of me, realizing that this kind of thing can happen to anybody. But it won't happen that way. In the end, her parents will blame me for Kat's near-overdose, even though I wasn't there when it happened. They'll tell the other neighborhood parents, "This kind of thing is contagious," like teenage pregnancy or suicide. They will refer to me as though I were the carrier drunk that had infected their children.

For all these reasons, a month of being grounded is a blessing. It allows time to pass, and people to forget about me. I imagine myself like the junkie bound for inpatient rehab, or somebody's pregnant daughter gone to Utah to give up the baby for adoption. I can emerge sometime in December in good health. I can come back from "visiting relatives" or that "much-needed break." One month is enough time for somebody else to replace me as the scapegoat for underage drinking. Surely someone else will do something stupid, and they will be strung up as a reminder to everyone else.

It doesn't take long. I rejoin the pack when an eleventh-grade girl, drunk on whiskey, puts a cigarette out on her ex-boyfriend's face. It allows me to sneak back into the game like someone who has been tossed out of dodgeball, in spite of being pronounced officially "out." I do it while the world is distracted, hurling its ammunition at somebody else.

From Social Drinker
to Alcoholic

Toren Volkmann

*Toren Volkmann shares his perspective on his alcohol depen-
dency, a problem that began in high school and increased during
his college years. In the following selection, he details his blackouts, hangovers, and terrifying encounters with alcohol withdrawal. He also relates his group therapy experience in a rehabilitation center, which prompts him to recollect his irresponsible
behavior during college and corresponding naivety about his addiction. Toren Volkmann grew up in Olympia, Washington. He
holds a bachelor's degree in psychology and has served as a volunteer in the Peace Corps, working in South America. He suc-
cessfully completed a six-month recovery program in a Florida
halfway house. In addition to writing, Volkmann enjoys compos-
ing and performing music.*

In Rehab

What the hell am I doing in rehab? I think I've always been a
pretty levelheaded guy, but I had a lot coming at me in my
first days back from my interrupted venture in South America
[as a volunteer in the Peace Corps]. Things had certainly
changed since the good old days. Being a part of the student
body at my university had given me license to party and get as
messed up as I wanted—as long as I held up my end of the
deal: objective, measurable results (grades) that justified the
absurd weekends, the ones that washed all that hearty education right out of my brain.

Who cares? I certainly didn't, and there wasn't anyone else
who would intervene, because most of my drinking (scary

enough) seemed normal, as long as you remember that any good drunk will surround himself with people who can party like rock stars as well. So what's the problem? I was a great student, from a great family, and I became a damn good volunteer. And don't question my motives in South America, because, by signing up, I wasn't avoiding my drinking, the real world, or the crap-ass job market. I entered the Peace Corps for other reasons.

Childhood Dreams

I've worked hard to paint such a bad-boy image of myself. I wasn't always this way. My decision to go into the Peace Corps stems from visions I'd had since I was young. I'd traveled with my family and experienced the beauty and cultural diversity offered in the world. As a child, I always dreamt of being a professional athlete, musician, and artist all in one lifetime— and a sensitive, fun-loving, and adventurous person, as well. I never envisioned I'd be the "I Told You So" poster boy for the D.A.R.E. [Drug Abuse Resistance Education] program.

When it came time to start making postcollege plans and decisions, the Peace Corps seemed like a worthy option. Although I realized I'd have to sacrifice countless familiarities, my cultural identity, my passion for the music scene, and everything else that rocked about being young in the good old United States of America, I felt I had a chance to learn another way of living, become a part of something bigger, and to potentially give back to a life that had given me everything. I might have been trying to maintain the course of my childhood dreams, but as a result of my drinking, all that I had ever envisioned hit the skids. Somewhere muddled up in my adolescence, "alcohol" and "ism" intermixed and my disease began to reveal itself.

So how did I land in rehab?

Denial

After being assessed by a professional in Washington, D.C., as a result of my desperate honesty (something new for me), I was told that I was an alcoholic and would need to go to an inpatient rehabilitation facility to learn about my disease and how to live with it. Screw that. Give me some therapy and some ways to deal with or control my drinking and put me on a plane back to South America. That's what I thought. With some tears and more negotiation, I figured I'd hold up my end of the deal, and after I was out of rehab and the doctors found out how great I was, how different, they'd just send me back to my wonderful life down in the hinterland. I am an exception, and always have been, right? *Denial.*

Group Therapy

My first day in group therapy, I told everyone my story, what brought me to rehab, how I always drank to get drunk, and that I felt that my withdrawal symptoms were getting so bad and unbearable that I'd asked for help. I was okay because I had known something was wrong and sought help of my own accord, right? I wasn't in denial. Besides, I looked around the place and saw all these crazy people with outrageous stories—addicts, lowlifes, winos—and I knew that I wasn't like them. I was fine. This center was full of people in pain, with damaged marriages or devastated families, pending charges and court orders, and all kinds of shame, guilt, and depression. These people were extremely sick.

When I was done and had shared my story, I felt pretty good about my situation and my honesty. We switched to some other people in the group and talked about some of their drinking, destructive habits, and behaviors. It was amazing how their denial completely disallowed them from seeing their own lives and drinking objectively and how their actions drastically affected other people. I thought it was insane. These guys had carted vodka into the office, had drunk on the way home from rehabs and detox centers, had countless DUIs [driving under the influence citations] or other offenses, had lost interest in their hobbies, and had destroyed many personal relationships. How could they not know they were alcoholics, that they had lost control, and that they were powerless over their substance? Their defenses were strong and they were in complete denial.

I'm Not in Denial

I wasn't in denial because I had asked for help and I came to rehab willingly. My story seemed so much better than most, and so clear to me. Since my blackouts and withdrawals were worsening, I was tired of it. So I figured rehab was necessary for the proper "adjustments." It felt good to finally talk about what had been bothering me for some time and it was easy for me to describe what worried me about my drinking. I didn't have any shame, guilt, or real consequences from my consumption. I drank purely for recreation, and whether I used alcohol to escape or not, well, who cares? The point is, I was doing it with all my good friends and we seemed to be just where we wanted to be.

Socially, alcohol had really seemed like a blessing to me, and the fact that I was in rehab angered me. I may have been able to use some help, but this was lame. I was able to shrug it off as another part of my story, and thought it would be a good learning experience.

"Hi, my name is Toren, and I'm an alcoholic." The first time I'd ever said that was in an AA meeting. I was nineteen and had just finished my freshman year of college. It really meant nothing to me in 1999. I said it with no ownership. I was there only because I was forced to be. I said it because everyone else said it, but it didn't apply to me at the time (so I thought). In 1999, at the end of my freshman year of college, my loving campus residence director (RD) told me that in order to be able to return to school the following fall, I would have to attend ten AA meetings and learn about the consequences of drinking and evaluate the seriousness of my problem. He told me, "Toren, I think you have a problem with alcohol." What the f— did he know?

Freshman Year in College

My freshman year had been one big celebration in a bottle, can, pill, pipe, or whatever seemed to fit or make itself available on that given Wednesday, Friday night, Sunday afternoon, or what have you. College life was a great chance to capitalize on everything that I had begun to excel at by the end of high school: having fun and not adhering to the rules or circumstances that applied to everyone else.

My first night in the dorms, before most people arrived, I unpacked and got settled in with blaring music and guzzled down about seven or eight ice beers, like any normal person would do. I was at home. The first time I met my residence assistant (RA), I was drinking beer out of a coffee mug. I mistook him for a regular student and kept drinking in front of him, until I realized who he was. He didn't catch me that time.

Breaking the Rules

Obviously, I hadn't planned to follow the rules from the start ... definitely not when it came to drinking. Coincidentally, I was put in a dorm with kids that shared my love for partying. In college? No kidding. We had a blast. Put a bunch of inventive college guys together and the outcome is almost a guarantee. I was in a single room and had no one to blame for all the behavioral issues that were to follow.

I lived in a dry part of campus, with all freshmen, but by the way I was drinking you wouldn't have guessed it. I was written up the first week for having alcohol in the dorm. By week four, I had been written up three different times for alcohol violations. I was penalized with fines that could be reduced by donating canned food. To pay my last fine, I came back to campus with two suitcases full of canned soups, vegetables, chili and beans. We joked that the RAs and RDs just sat around and ate it all themselves.

The second time I was caught, I was forced to go to a "second offenders meeting" with a few other kids who had also been caught twice. It was early in the year, so the counselors asked why we were getting caught like we did, and what would help us stay out of trouble. They asked why we drank so much, and wondered if alcohol-free student activities were lacking on campus, as if maybe that was part of the problem. To me, the problem was that I kept getting caught. I decided to ensure that it didn't happen again.

Getting Caught

My third offense was a week later, proving all my efforts were in vain. I was the first freshman to have a "third offenders meeting," and attended it alone with only counselors. I no longer thought it was funny. For different reasons, the counselors thought it was pretty serious, too. But screw them all. The rules were too strict. The RAs weren't fair and were going after or picking on certain people. I just had bad luck. I'd be damned if I was going to mellow out—this was college, for God's sake.

With my new buddies, I made frequent trips to a big grocery store and got kicks out of sneaking cheap handles of vodka, forties, tall cans of malt liquor, and glorious half racks of shitty ice beers back into the dorms. Always giddy and excited, we exercised our freedom to celebrate or abuse every chance we got, and that was often. Excessive drinking led to plenty of random acts of chaos, the occasional trash-can fire or petty vandalism, or general insanity. It was all fun and games and no one got hurt. With more and more write-ups on our floor, and empties collecting outside our entryway, ours became a marked building.

The unpredictable fire drills we set off required the whole building to evacuate in the middle of the night. Watching tired and unprepared students file out was icing on the cake. It was a joke to us. I guess no one else enjoyed it on as many levels as we did. The staff surely didn't. Their attempts to control us seemed to make us wilder and more rebellious, and we ate it up. It was an exciting time for a bunch of "serious" students.

Of course, I didn't divulge any real information about my behaviors to the counselors or other residential-life staff. I maintained innocence, and I continued to play the bad-luck card. Even though I had already tallied my third offense, they still wanted to believe me. I was fine. I cited my good grades as proof. It seemed convincing.

As a result of my third offense, I had several meetings with the RAs and RD. My drinking was assessed in a confidential meeting. I met with a counselor one-on-one and was asked about my drinking style and the choices I was making for myself. I suppose this was all part of my intervention process, but I didn't give it a fair chance. For the most part I knew that certain behaviors would indicate risky drinking or problem drinking, so I toned down my answers and shaved the numbers regarding how much and how often when talking about my drinking habits. I wasn't into the whole honesty thing.

The staff on campus wanted me to take a look at my drinking. They said it was serious. All I wanted was for them to lay off me, and for me to be able to do what I wanted. Was that so much to ask?

Unable to Stay Out of Trouble

My grades were outstanding that fall, as were my party achievements. Although crazy and belligerent for the most part, I managed my time well. I played hard, but I studied hard, too. I even made the dean's list. But by spring, my standing on campus had gotten pretty ugly. I couldn't stay out of trouble. I was a victim of unwanted and what I perceived as unfair attention by the campus police. After being relocated away from most of my friends and moved up onto the main campus, I was given fair warning. No more violations or setting foot on the lower portion of campus, or I was out.

Still, I had only bad things to say about all the snooty people on the campus and the nothing-better-to-do Public Safety Team. They patrolled past my door constantly, and, on weekends, even checked the balcony with a spotlight in order to make sure there were no shenanigans happening after hours. I was pretty fed up at this point with all these authority figures on their high horses telling me what to do and singling me out. I wasn't the only minor drinking, on or off campus, and I sure as hell didn't need my hand held during my adjustment to college life—my grades were fine.

Motivation for College

I continued to push buttons, bend rules, and enjoy my first year of college as I pleased. I managed to remain on campus, although barely, the entire year. While my grades began to suffer a bit that spring, I was also working part-time for dining services setting up snacks and drink bars for big-money conferences and helping to cater special events on campus. The occasional complimentary wine was nice and made me less resentful of the weak-ass paychecks. In my last meeting with the RD, we had a serious chat. The cumulative behavior and damage was enough, I guess. He understood in some way that a lot of people have problems adjusting to college and that maybe it would be good for me to reevaluate my motivation for being in school.

My motivation? I was there to have fun, party, meet new people, and, of course, to get that pricey degree—in four years or under.

Walking a Fine Line

My parents were paying for my education, not for my exploitation of college life, and it was my job to perform in school in order to stay. I was walking a fine line and my parents were always at the other end with their radar, questions, concerns, and, thankfully, their support and unconditional love. It was tough to satisfy my own expectations, my parents' expectations, and all those people catching my slipups. No one from the college contacted my parents or informed them what I'd been up to.

The RD told me that in order for me to return, there had to be some major changes in my attitude. My current behavior would not be allowed. What he couldn't understand was how I could seem like such a reasonable person during the day, yet get caught twice publicly urinating in the same spot— the second time out of drunken spite. Why was it like dealing with an angel in our face-to-face meetings and like dealing with the devil at night when I was confronted by Public Safety? My answer was simple: those bastards were always following us around, trying to catch or control us, and we just wanted to do what normal college kids are doing everywhere. Therefore, I didn't like Public Safety, and I let them know it at certain times.

Surprisingly, this brilliant answer didn't really cut it. I would not be allowed to live on campus the following year. The RD said it was a shame that sometimes some of the brightest kids with the most potential seemed to cause the most trouble and find themselves with the most problems. I thought it was a shame that he was a forty-year-old man living in the dorms, babysitting a bunch of college kids and penalizing them for their basic right to have fun. I felt that we students were completely justified in raging and spending our youth and invincibility while we had it. He also told me to go to those AA meetings. What a joker. He didn't know who I was.

This attitude of mine did not crop up overnight. I had always felt indestructible, and reacted pretty sarcastically to the whole notion of being an alcoholic. Even back in high school, I remember being sixteen or seventeen, drinking beers with a couple of friends and mockingly reading through one of those typical self-help pamphlets. We were checking the one or more drinking behaviors that applied to us (in my case, there were many more). If I remember right, exhibiting only a few of those behaviors signified that you were probably an alcoholic. I remember laughing, as we were pounding beers, because one of the questions asked if we ever "drank faster in certain situations or thought that we took bigger than average gulps at times." Our response was, of course, "Hell yeah we do, how else would we do it?" That was the only way we did it. I proudly exhibited pretty much every indicator. But I felt like I was doing most of them intentionally. I drank to get drunk. I thought it was hilarious, and never once considered that someday that kind of drinking might not be a choice. In short, that is how I landed in rehab.

Sometime after my momentous freshman year of college, I bought a cheesy greeting card on a whim because it caught my eye, and sent it to my brother. Along with this last-minute card I probably sent a letter, or some pictures or newspaper clippings. On the front of the card was a big bottle of champagne with celebratory glasses and colorful balloons splashed with confetti going everywhere. Right over the top, in fancy writing, it read *"Congratulations!"* Inside, the card was blank. But what I wrote there typified my attitude and glorification of drunkenness at the time: *"You're a Flaming Alcoholic!"* I thought it was the funniest thing in the world and sent it off to my brother.

Sure. My brothers and I took pride in drinking like alcoholics. I guess in some ways, I shouldn't have been so surprised to find myself in rehab, after all.

While I was in treatment, that same brother sent me a letter, doing his best to be supportive and sensitive. It's too bad he didn't include that same card with his letter. It would have been so much more appropriate for me. "Congratulations! *You're* a Flaming Alcoholic!" I wonder if the idea ever crossed his mind.

CHAPTER 2

Coping with a Parent's Addiction

The Challenges of Living with an Alcoholic Mother

Rishon Roberts, as told to Sandy Fertman Ryan

Fifteen-year-old Rishon Roberts has lived with her father since she was a year old due to her mother's alcoholism. At twelve and looking for a closer relationship, Roberts decided to move in with her mother. Roberts soon discovered the challenges and disappointment of living with her alcoholic mother: Her mom was unreliable, constantly drinking, and behaving irresponsibly and inappropriately. Roberts was ashamed of her mother's disease and hid this secret from friends. Before finishing eighth grade, Roberts grew tired of having to play the parent role and decided to move back with her father. Roberts has found a sense of inner strength and independence after living with her mother. Using her experience to help others, Roberts has volunteered at a teen crisis counseling center, talking to kids with similar problems.

Learning Mom Is an Alcoholic

I've honestly never felt sorry for myself for not having my mom around when I was younger. I think it's because my dad is so amazing. I've lived with him from the time I was a year old. He never sat me down to explain why I couldn't live with my mom but, over the years, I figured out that she is an alcoholic.

It wasn't until I was 12, though, that I finally understood what "alcoholism" actually means. Up until then, I didn't think it was all that big of a deal—I just didn't have any idea how dangerous this disease really is.

Rishon Roberts, as told to Sandy Fertman Ryan, "Bottled Emotions," *Girls' Life*, vol. 13, December 2006, Copyright © 2006 *Girls' Life*. All rights reserved. Reproduced by permission.

My brother and I usually visited my mom about six times a year. She must have been careful to hide the disease from us—I have no memory of seeing her drink, and our visits were nice.

Moving in with Mom

By the end of sixth grade, I noticed my friends talked a lot about their moms. They'd say things like, "My mom took me shopping, and it was so much fun!" I found myself feeling kind of envious. It was weird not to be able to do things with my mom like other kids. Still, I tried to put it out of my mind.

But soon, I was so curious about what it would be like to live with my mom. I wanted to have the kind of relationship with her my friends had with their moms. I went to my dad one day when I was 12 and said, "I'd really like to go live with Mom for a while." My dad was really shocked and said, "Are you sure?"

When it was nearing the time for me to move to my mom's house and begin seventh grade, he asked again. I think he was worried about how my mom's behavior might affect me. He told me he didn't think it was a good idea for me to go but that he wasn't going to stop me.

I knew my mom was irresponsible and had serious problems, but I had to try. My brother decided to live with my mom, too, which was cool but also sort of sad. We'd both lived with my dad our entire lives, and I was afraid it would hurt him to lose us both. But my dad was totally supportive, as usual.

Drunk Again

I'd never spent time around an alcoholic, so I didn't have a *clue* what I was in for. Almost immediately, I noticed my mom drank alcohol every single day, which was shocking to me. She'd start with wine and beer at about 11 A.M. From that point on, I never saw her without a drink in her hand.

The first time I saw her get really drunk was at a beach bonfire with her friends. She was really loud and obnoxious, and it was uncomfortable seeing her act that way. She just didn't seem "mom-like," and I hated it. I was finally trying to have a mother-daughter relationship . . . and she was acting like a teen.

Although my mom was never mean to me, she could definitely say mean things to other people. She didn't care about anyone when she was drunk.

I couldn't stand being near her when she'd been drinking. It was like she was a stranger, and that was disgusting to me. From the beginning, I felt like I was the mom and she was the kid—and I was only 12. Because she was so unreliable. I had to cook, clean and do all the other "mom stuff." That was tough because I had school, too. I wanted to be the kid again. I quickly learned the only way to deal with my home life was to go to my room and shut the door or stay at friends' houses, which I did a lot.

My mom and I often argued when she was drinking, but it was always about absolutely nothing, which was frustrating. Our conversations were stupid. She'd assume things about my life or gossip about my teachers, and it drove me nuts because she knew nothing about me. She was too busy drinking.

I never told my mom outright that I couldn't stand her drinking habit because I knew we would fight about it. I kept it to myself and occasionally commented so she'd know how I felt. There was nothing I could do about it anyway.

It took a seventh-grade science class to clue me in on the exact nature of alcoholism. My teacher explained that it is hereditary, and I thought, "What?! *I* could become an alcoholic?" That scared me. I also learned that my mom can't help craving alcohol since it is a disease. But I was still mad at my mom. I figured if she loved me, she would just stop.

I've tasted alcohol, but I don't like it. I'm not saying I'll never do it again, but I don't care about it at all. And I'll always be aware of the fact that I'm more likely than others to become an alcoholic. But drinking reminds me of my mom and how awful she made me feel, so I hope I'll never let that happen to me.

My Little Secret

I was too ashamed to talk to my friends about my mom's problem. It was like a terrible secret. But my best friend Erica figured it out. She'd see my mom act weird, but we never really talked about it. Looking back, I realize it was hard to hold in all of that shame. I shouldn't have. It probably made things worse.

Fortunately, my grades didn't suffer. My mom was never successful, so I wanted to prove myself by doing well in school. Plus, school was a great escape. I avoided going home after school because I never knew what to expect.

I don't blame myself for my mom's drinking, but it definitely damaged my self-esteem. Whenever my friends came over or I had to go out with my mom, I was worried about how she would behave. When we went to back-to-school night, my mom acted ridiculous. She always dressed too young, wearing low-cut tops. But, at the same time, I felt really guilty for being ashamed of her. I mean, she's still my mom. I love her.

My mom was nice to my friends, but she fought with my stepdad in front of them. So by eighth grade, I avoided having friends over. Pretty soon, I heard school gossip like, "Don't expect Rishon to invite you over!" I thought, "Well, there's a good reason for that, but I'm not going to tell you what it is." It was incredibly awkward—and humiliating—knowing kids were talking about me.

When I went to my friends' houses, their moms always treated me like *they* were my mom. That was comforting, and it helped keep me sane.

Time to Leave

Living with my mom was a huge let-down. I had planned to stay with her through high school. A few weeks before eighth grade ended, I realized I had to go. I was sitting at the dinner table with my mom and brother, and I said, "I'm moving back home." My mom cried and said, "No, you're going to high school here!" We had a huge fight, but I'd made up my mind.

My brother stayed, and I knew he could take care of himself. But I was sad to leave my friends. I had wanted to finish high school with them. But I wasn't at all sad to leave my room. I was way too angry. I knew she loved me, but she loved alcohol just as much. That hurt.

I was relieved when I got home. I didn't have to *be* the mom anymore. My dad and stepmom were completely there for me, and I was grateful to have them.

A Shaky Future

One day after I had moved, my mom was speeding on the freeway and hit a tree. She wasn't injured, but she was charged with driving under the influence of alcohol and sentenced to house arrest for six months. During that time, she was required to stay sober. But as soon as her sentence was up, she and my stepdad took me out to celebrate—and my mom ordered a *margarita*! I couldn't believe it. I was like, "Are you crazy?!" I thought this was her chance to get clean.

Since then, my brother claims she's doing a bit better, but I'm uncertain about her future. I think it would take something extreme, like her getting injured or injuring someone else, for her to get treatment. It's sad to think she might never get help, but it's up to her.

The Silver Lining

Some positive things have come from the time I spent with my mom. It made me stronger and independent. And it makes me determined to never be like her. I feel proud for having survived such a horrible experience.

If you have a parent who is an alcoholic, talk to someone about it. Keeping it inside never helps. Confide in someone you trust, or call a teen crisis line. I now do phone crisis counseling at Teen-Line in Los Angeles to help other kids with similar problems and, surprisingly, it's helped me. I'm not alone. Everyone, at some time, has difficulties in life.

I'll keep praying my mom gets help, even though things don't look so great. Still, I know there's always hope.

My Mother Is an Alcoholic

Cortney Philip

Cortney Philip is the daughter of a functional alcoholic. In the following selection, she describes her mother's ability to hide her drinking problem and admits that she has kept her mother's alcoholism a secret for many years out of embarrassment. As she has matured, however, Philip has become more confident in her decision to abstain from alcohol and more comfortable acknowledging her mother's illness. She offers young people advice on how to get help. Through the assistance of support groups, she has realized that she no longer needs to feel isolated and ashamed just because her mother is an alcoholic.

My mother is an alcoholic. She has been one for as long as I can remember, and probably even longer than that. As far as appearances go, you'd never guess that she has a serious problem. She dresses nicely, has lots of friends, and always shows up for work on time. She's what most would call a functional alcoholic, someone who can hide the damaging effects of alcohol on their health and personal life. In my mother's case, that means that she seems pretty ordinary; she doesn't start drinking until she gets home from work, but she is drunk by 9:00 every night.

A Shameful Secret

Addiction in a family causes problems with day-to-day life. For example, I loved spending the night at my friends' houses, because their families seemed so healthy compared to mine. As much as I wanted to, though, I couldn't invite anyone to spend the night at my house. It was too embarrassing to let my friends see my mother after she'd been drinking for a few hours.

Cortney Philip, "My Mother Is an Alcoholic," *Listen*, vol. 59, no. 6, February 2006, pp. 4–5. Reproduced by permission of the author.

Sitting through drug and alcohol prevention classes in school made me feel nervous, because my mother's alcohol use was a secret I was ashamed of. My friends and I were proud of the fact that we abstained from drugs and alcohol, and I didn't want anyone to know that someone in my own home was addicted to alcohol.

Staying Clean

As I got older, it became even more important to me to stay away from drugs and alcohol, especially because I knew that it would be easy for me to end up like my mother. Alcohol was always available in my house, and it took a lot of willpower to abstain when most people I knew were experimenting. However, it also became easier to talk to people about my mother and not feel judged. I found out that some of the people I liked and respected also had loved ones with alcohol and drug abuse problems, and it didn't make them bad people. It was just something we lived with and learned from.

Take It from Me

If someone you love has a problem with drugs or alcohol, there are things you can do to help. First, make a list of ways that substance abuse affects you because of the choices your loved one is making. Simply knowing that it hurts you could help them make a step toward quitting. Unfortunately, my mother was unable to quit drinking, although she tried many times. But because I'd let her know that some of her actions affected me negatively, we worked out a system to keep me safe. For example, when I went somewhere after school, we decided it would be much better if I walked home or got a ride from someone else. That way, neither one of us was in danger of getting into an alcohol-related accident.

Help Is Available

There are many support groups for people who want to quit drinking or using drugs. Many people are too afraid to go to that first meeting, but you could offer to go and lend your loving support. Alcoholics Anonymous and Narcotics Anonymous are so big that almost every town has a meeting at least once a week. These meetings openly welcome new members. They promise to keep your identity truly anonymous.

To find an Alcoholics Anonymous or Narcotics Anonymous meeting in your area, look in your telephone book or community events sections of newspapers. If you and your loved one cannot attend a meeting in person, meetings are also held online. Some meetings are closed to the public. Meetings that are open to supporters will be listed as either "open speaker meetings" or "open discussion meetings."

If your loved one is unable or unwilling to get help, there are support groups for you, too. If you need a ride and call ahead, you can probably get someone from the group to drive you, even if you have never been before. Remember, these groups are there to help you in whatever way you need, and a support group may be a place you can feel comfortable talking about what you're going through. Children of alcoholics and drug users are more likely than others to develop addictions later in life, and a support group can help you to be strong enough to abstain from abusing drugs.

Alateen meetings are for teens who have friends or family who are alcoholics. New members are always welcome to observe and attend meetings. No one will tell your school or your family you have been there, even if you are under 18. Meetings and local chapter phone numbers are listed online.

Learning from Others

The most important thing to remember is that you are your own person. Nobody can take the decision to abstain from drugs and alcohol away from you. You don't have to be alone or embarrassed. Although my mother is still an alcoholic, I've learned from others that it is OK to love her without being ashamed or making bad decisions for myself.

My Mother's Sober Year

Lee Montgomery

Lee Montgomery recalls her mother's singular experience with sobriety in the year 1969. In the following excerpt from her memoir about living in an alcoholic household, she reconstructs the events surrounding her mother's brief and reluctant decision to quit drinking. She remembers her thoughts and feelings as a twelve-year-old, spending quality time with her mother for the first, and only, time before her mother reverted to a life of substance abuse. Montgomery is an executive editor at Tin House *magazine and editorial director of the Tin House Books division. She lives in Portland, Oregon.*

Mother's First Drink of the Day

First things first. You have to meet my mother. You have to meet the Mumzy in the morning, sitting with her old tree root legs, stunted and worn, dangling off the edge of the king-size bed she shares with my father. In front of her is a purple walker, reminiscent of a racing bicycle with four wheels, its wire basket stuffed with socks, notebooks, a Kleenex or two. She looks up at the clock that sings a different bird song every hour on the hour and announces to my father, who is reading in a chair, "Monty, it is eight forty-five." She holds up three fingers to indicate the number of ounces of gin she wants in her drink. My father leaves the room, and I study my mother's face, the folds in her skin collapsed around bones and things she cannot express. I pat her shoulder and follow my father into the other room to watch him make my mother a drink— one of his many chores since Mother broke her shoulder a few years earlier.

In the kitchen an old wooden chest of my grandfather's stores booze and nuts and crackers. My father flips open the top, reaches into its belly to pull out a half-gallon jug of Tanqueray, and pours it into a jigger twice. There is something disconnected about his movements, but he says nothing. The only sounds come from the clinking of glass and ice and the pouring of spirits.

I am following my father around my childhood home now—watching, studying—because the doctors recently found the reason that he has been losing weight and, in the last few weeks, has found it difficult to swallow: He has a tumor in his stomach. They do not know if it is malignant or not, which is why I study him so vigilantly; I am trying to decipher our future.

Dad reaches into the fridge and grabs a handful of fresh mint, and from a cabinet, a few plastic straws, and stuffs the bunch into the glass. He knows I watch him so he completes this maneuver with a self-conscious flair. "Take that!"

My father and I deliver Mother's drink and sit silently. I lie back on the lavender carpet and stretch my back, sneaking peeks at both of them. My mother, sitting on the edge of the bed, stares out the French doors into the field and my father goes back to his paperback thriller. The black pancake face of their little dog, Inky, peeks out from under the bed, and while I pat her, I pull at an odd tumor, a sac of skin, that hangs off her neck. Mom looks at Dad and then at me sadly, her expression asking, *Now what do we do?* I smile at her, trying to be reassuring, as I am thinking *Dunno. Dunno. Dunno.*

Three days earlier, on a bright autumn morning, Mom and Pop call with the news.

"But the test says no cancer?" I say into the phone. "That's good, isn't it?"

"Partly sunny, partly cloudy," Dad says. "It's the same damn thing. There's still a tumor there."

According to my father, they can't identify the tumor because "the asshole" on the other end of the scope can't get a piece of the thing to analyze. When he says this, all I can think about is the doctor. I had known his daughter in kindergarten. I remember her especially well because I had adored her mother, particularly how she made tuna sandwiches. I'd never seen anyone do anything so mundane with such care. She used Miracle Whip, not mayonnaise, and toasted the bread, cutting off the crusts, and slicing the beautiful remainder into tiny triangles.

"Please come," Mother says from the other extension.

"What is she going to do, Barbara?" my father says.

"You need support."

"I DO NOT need support."

"I do, then," she says.

"I need the kids available if I have to have surgery," my father says. "There's no point. . . ."

"F— it," I finally say. "I'm coming."

"Jesus," my father says. "Your language is awful. You take after your mother."

"Go to hell," my mother says.

Dad says nothing, but hell is where I'm headed. I climb on a plane and fly east, back to Framingham and my parents' home.

The Year My Mother Was Sober

Of all the years I live with my parents, my mother is sober for only one. It is 1969, the year of Woodstock. The year the men first walk on the moon. For our family, it is the year Mother dresses up in miniskirts and white go-go boots and smokes Kools. She wears false eyelashes the size of carpet remnants and drinks Tab by the case. She cuts her bleached blond hair in the style that Twiggy has made popular, and brings crazy people home from the back wards of the state mental hospital where she is a volunteer.

There is a schizophrenic drummer, a millionaire paranoid depressive, and a manic-depressive from the CIA, who, comparatively speaking, is a relief. I am twelve that summer, and honing my cooking skill, so I make lunch while Mother drives to pick up the lunatics. I usually make hamburgers with Swiss cheese, sliced purple onion, sweet pickles and corn relish, and chocolate milkshakes. We serve them in the dining room on paper plates. I try to make conversation while I watch the crazy people eat. Everything about them is strange, but to my mind, crazy people are thrilling, even slightly glamorous—like my mother.

The schizophrenic drummer ate too much LSD in Vietnam. When he talks, he mumbles into his chest. The millionaire is too depressed to talk. He is fat and his eyes are scarily weird. He wears his hair in a mental-patient crew cut, his pants hang around his hips, and he shuffles along looking at the floor. But the CIA guy, who apparently lost it after hearing about a plot to kill someone he knew and even loved, is enthusiastic as hell, like a Labrador retriever. He babbles incessantly about everything. He is six feet tall, a handsome dandy who likes horses. He dresses in tweed with leather elbow patches, jodhpurs, and jodhpur boots, and talks in a faux British accent, as if he has marbles in his mouth. For a short time, these are our friends.

Forced into Sobriety

It isn't Mother's idea to get sober. It's a decision that results from something that happened the previous year, the year of Johnny Mathis. He had recently come out with a new album, *Up Up and Away*. My mother loved to stay up all night and drink gin martinis and sing along with Johnny Mathis. She wrote down the lyrics in spiral-lined notebooks and practiced the melodies for days, recording them into a professional reel-to-reel tape recorder, pretending she was Judy Garland.

One morning after she has stayed up all night with Johnny Mathis, I find her passed out in a pool of blood in the downstairs bathroom, her eye bloody and swollen. At least that's where I think I find her, but when I try to picture my mother lying on the bathroom floor, the image dissolves. It's Jezebel the mink who throws me off. Jezebel was a gift from a neighboring mink farmer, a skinny fellow who has spindly teeth and resembles a mink himself. Her cage was in the bathroom, and I am now not sure there was enough room for both the cage and my mother on the floor. Maybe she isn't fully on the floor but curled around the toilet or I might have made it up. Maybe I find her on the living room floor. My mother's amnesiac cloud permeates me, too; life from these years remains hazy.

Though I am now unclear on physical details, at the time I am oddly excited. The drama of a real accident! Suddenly, all the chaos that has defined my world has something concrete to attach to. Her fall confirms a reality that is only occasionally acknowledged. Mother is a drunk, but a drunk who dreams about traveling with Johnny Mathis makes the truth more palatable: *At least she is glamorous.*

My father wraps her up and takes her to the emergency room at the local hospital. When they return later that morning, Mother's head is bandaged and angry voices bellow from behind the closed doors of the kitchen. It must be summer because my older brother Bob is home from college. He and Dad corner her. Get sober or we're taking you away. Where? Westborough State Hospital. An incredible insult. An undeniable kick in the teeth. We all know anybody who is anybody would be packed off to McLean's, where it was rumored the real rich paid more than $1000 a day. We aren't the real rich. We are the *once sort of* rich a long time ago, which, according to Mother, is better.

My mother corroborates my version of the event, referring to it for years as the time she went up, up and away in Johnny's beautiful balloon and crashed. She laughs as she says it. My father laughs, too. Ha! He laughs! She laughs! I laugh with them. My older sister, Lael, shakes her head and says, "Oh, brother." Bob screws up his face and says, "Jesus Christ."

There is a saying that my father begins to use around this time: "For Christ's sakes, Barbara, do you have to be such a horse's ass?"

And Mother? What does she say? "You tell 'em horse shit, you've been on the road."

Pretending to Have a Normal Mother

Besides our new friends and the miniskirts, at first everything stays the same. Dad, still an engineer salesman with the cumbersome title of "manufacturers representative," spends his days driving up and down Route 128, selling widgets to the aerospace industry. Lael, only twenty-one, married a Navy ensign the year before and is living on a Navy base in Athens, Georgia. Bob is in his second year at the Rhode Island School of Design, which leaves me, the youngest at twelve, home, alone, riding my pony Happy Birthday around in circles, watching this mysterious woman who claims to be my mother click around in go-go boots towing a band of loonies.

We work hard to make it work. We walk on eggshells. We hold our breath waiting for the other shoe to drop. In the meantime, I spend the year pretending I have a mother who is normal—*sort of*. She begins to do mother-like things. We spend afternoons picking blueberries. We bake Jordan Marsh muffins and pies with recipes with secret ingredients for flakey piecrusts given to us by our neighbor. We chase Johnny Mathis, me following Mother as she tries to get backstage under a big circus tent next to the first mall in America, Shoppers' World, in Framingham, the town we live in. Mother knits cabled sweaters at startling speeds. We take a plane to see my sister in Georgia. We ride together. My parents take photographs. Mother buys me a fancy Steuben saddle and shows me how to braid my pony's mane and tail with a needle and thread. All these events seem mundane, normal, like life in an all-American family.

The balloon crash is the only time I remember my father taking a visible stand against Mother's drinking. Before this year, and after it too, my father silently endures, assuming both parenting roles. He takes me shopping for school clothes and party shoes, ferries me to and from dancing school, and watches me in recitals and class plays. Outside of that year, Mother has the dubious distinction of missing every event of my life, including graduations and my wedding.

So, I'll always be grateful to Johnny Mathis and his balloon. Nineteen sixty-nine is the sole year I look at my mother and feel something like pride. She is beautiful. She wears long dungaree coats, safari suits, and stylish straw hats. But like all good things, it is short-lived. By the summer of 1970, the lights go out again.

CHAPTER 3

Alcoholism from the Perspective of Family and Friends

A Lonely Addict Reaches Out

Jean Thompson

Jean Thompson reminisces about her friend, Ben, a writer and alcoholic who died in a fatal drunk-driving accident. In the following selection, she considers their after-hours phone conversations, during which Ben would read his most recent compositions, and probes the significance of their conversations in light of her friend's drinking problem. She concludes that through her own writing, she can honor Ben's memory. Thompson is a novelist and short story writer living in Urbana, Illinois. Her short fiction collection Who Do You Love *was a finalist for the National Book Award. Her novel* Wide Blue Yonder *was selected as a* New York Times *Notable Book and was one of the* Chicago Tribune's *picks for Best Fiction of 2002. She has received fellowships from both the National Endowment for the Arts and the Guggenheim Foundation.*

Late Night Phone Calls

Back then, my phone would ring at 1 or 2 o'clock in the morning, and Ben's voice would be in my ear. No greeting or preamble, just the crackle of his notebook's pages and the words unspooling. That was what he liked to do, ambush me with a story, jump out of the darkness and mug me with it. "It's Ben," I'd whisper to my boyfriend, who'd groan himself back to sleep. I'd listen for however long he read, sometimes drifting off, or trying gamely to follow along and make appreciative noises.

There was a two-hour time difference between Ben out in Washington State and me in the Midwest. I imagined he'd started drinking in the late afternoon, with his kids making a racket and his wife keeping order as she tended to dinner. Ben would tell a joke he'd told a dozen times, just to make the youngest child laugh. As the night wore on, the wave of good feeling from the drinking would crest and recede little by little, until Ben sat alone in his bright empty kitchen with a bottle and the phone. But he never sounded drunk; he gave each word its proper weight. His voice carried me with it. Then he'd stop. Story over. The silence traveling miles over whistling black wires stretched across the Rockies and all those lonesome farm states. My cue to speak. "Good stuff, Ben."

"Honest opinion. Don't pussyfoot, O.K.?"

No, I'd protest, I liked this or that part. I was awake by then, but Ben would have slipped another notch toward alcoholic stupor. His breath was a half snore. "Good night, Ben."

He'd rouse himself. "Hey, love you guys. Really. Love ya."

Witnessing a Friend's Drinking Problem

I wasn't always happy to get those calls, didn't always feel like humoring Ben or losing sleep. You can't witness someone's problem drinking, even from a distance, without exasperation. But there's a reservoir of good will for longtime friends that takes a while to run dry. And besides, they were fine stories, about his home, the West, the dusty roads and dry bent-grass hills and basalt cliffs, about driving out before dawn to hunt ducks, the sweet, aching mysteries of the poky little towns. You can put up with a lot for a good story.

We'd started out together as young writers, beginners, Ben and I, although he was 10 years older, had already been in the Army, married and started a family. So there was always more at stake for him in wanting to be a writer, more riding on his success or failure. If alcohol and writers are such a notorious pairing, it's because drinking is one way you can bluff yourself into believing you just might make it, something to fill the awful space of the blank page. What reason is there to be a writer? The world is perfectly cheerful about the prospect of your never being one.

Ben the Happy Drunk

We all drank a lot in those days. None of us had heard about denial or enabling or the rest of that soon-to-be-common language. We had yet to suffer any casualties. Ben was most often a happy drunk, generous, wanting to buy you a drink or a pizza or invite you over to the house. But one night, when a group had gathered in someone's living room to talk about our stories, he got himself liquored up beforehand. Maybe it was to take the edge off the terrible anxiety of having his work judged. He interrupted the discussion, a serious breach of etiquette. "What do you mean you don't like it? That's bull." His mouth set in a grin that was ready to tighten and grow ugly.

There must have been something safe in those late-night calls, something anonymous and holy about sending his words to me, the only woman in our group, the little sister who had yet to come into her own as a writer or to learn that you don't have to accommodate drunks. If he had lived long enough, that friendship might have changed and become one more thing lost in the war between Ben's best and worst selves.

We made one trip out West to see Ben and his family. He cooked up batches of "the best damn nachos in the world" and fed us home-kippered salmon and scrambled eggs. In my memory everyone is happy, and for that visit, drinking and all, it was still the good old days. Ben couldn't stop laughing when I told him the corn in his garden was puny by Midwest standards. He had a roaring laugh that put high color in his face and made his foxy mustache bristle. It was the last time I ever saw him.

The Death of a Friend

With some stories, you can see the end coming. I have a letter from him in which he talked about how good he was feeling since he'd quit drinking, how he was working out every day. It didn't last. There were the kinds of struggles that are too familiar to interest anyone, except when they happen to somebody you love. And then one night the phone rang in the darkness, but it wasn't Ben. It was his wife, telling me that he had been out drinking, missed a curve driving and hit a tree head-on. His chest was crushed, and he died instantly. I hung up and looked out through the dark west window. It was a long time ago. One reason to be a writer is for your friends who no longer can be.

The Impact of Codependency and Addiction

Robert Burney

Robert Burney reflects on the death of his friend, Robert, whom he met in treatment for alcoholism. In the following selection, he analyzes his friend's dysfunctional self-image, as well as the emotional, mental, and spiritual implications of his friend's inability to remain sober. Burney asserts that despite the genetic component of alcoholism, it was his friend's codependence—his internal spiritual battle and his failure to love and trust himself—that ultimately took his life. Robert Burney is a therapist and spiritual instructor specializing in codependency. He is the author of Codependence: The Dance of Wounded Souls *and the creator of Joy to You and Me Enterprises, a web-based resource center on codependency and recovery.*

As long as we look outside of Self—with a capital S—to find out who we are, to define ourselves and give us self-worth, we are setting ourselves up to be victims.

We were taught to look outside of ourselves—to people, places, and things; to money, property, and prestige—for fulfillment and happiness. It does not work, it is dysfunctional. We cannot fill the hole within with anything outside of Self.

You can get all the money, property, and prestige in the world, have everyone in the world adore you, but if you are not at peace within, if you don't Love and accept yourself, none of it will work to make you Truly happy. *Codependence: The Dance of Wounded Souls* by Robert Burney.

My friend Robert died the other day. He died alone in a hotel room and his body wasn't found for two days. He weighed 125 pounds when he died.

Robert Burney, "The Death of an Alcoholic," http://www.silcom.com, Reproduced by permission.

Robert's Drinking

Robert was an alcoholic who couldn't stay sober. He had been through full thirty day (and longer) treatment programs at least 15 times. He had been in detox fifty times easily. Drinking had destroyed his body. Robert should have been dead years ago. In the past 3 or 4 years almost every time he drank he ended up in intensive care. I did much of my grieving for my friend three years ago, the last time I rescued him from his cabin on Taos Mountain and took him to the emergency room.

Robert went to lots of meetings and tried real hard to work the program but on one critical point he didn't have enough humility. He did not have enough humility to accept that he was lovable.

Robert Felt Unworthy of Love

My friend had made and lost fortunes in his life. He had been with lots of women and had lots of possessions. He still had lots of possessions when he died. He still had the cabin in Taos Ski Valley but he didn't have the strength to walk up the fifty steps to the front door.

Robert used money to try to buy friendship and love. And then he felt betrayed because he believed that people only wanted to be around him for his money. If you were friendly to him for no apparent reason then he would talk about giving you money because that gave you an excuse to care about him. He just could not believe that he was worthy of love just for who he was.

Robert Was Filled with Shame

Robert was full of shame. He was full of shame because he was raised in a dysfunctional family in a shame-based society. His Father was a verbally/emotionally abusive perfectionist for whom nothing was ever good enough. His mother was too terrified and shame-based to protect her son. As a young child

Robert got the message that he wasn't lovable but that if he was successful enough and made enough money he might earn the right to be loved. He was successful and made lots of money but it did not work to convince him that he was good enough.

My friend had no permission from himself to receive love. When I published my book I listed him among people who had touched my life on the Acknowledgements Page. When he saw his name listed there he cursed me (his generation, and mine, were taught to relate to other men that way, to say 'I love you' by calling each other names) and cried briefly (which he felt was very shameful) and then he drank. In his relationship with himself Robert was too shame-based to believe that he was lovable.

Genetic Predisposition Toward Alcoholicism

I believe that the great majority of Alcoholics are born with a genetic, hereditary predisposition that is physiological. Environment does not cause Alcoholism. Robert was not an Alcoholic because he was shame-based—it was because of his shame that he could not stay sober. He had a blustery, 'hail-fellow-well-met', in your face kind of ego-strength that was very fragile. As soon as he got sober his ego defenses would fracture and the shame underneath would cause him to sabotage his sobriety.

That doesn't mean that people who can stay sober don't have shame. Some of us just have more ego defenses that buries the shame deeper. That is good news in early sobriety because it helps one to stay sober. It can be bad news later on because it can cause us to resist growth and to not have the humility to be teachable. The reason that I am alive today is because I was able to go to treatment for Codependence in my fifth year of recovery while working as a therapist in a treatment center. I had sworn that I would kill myself before I drank again and the feelings which were surfacing had me close to it when I went to Sierra Tucson. That was where I met Robert.

Codependency and Alcoholism: Two Fatal Diseases

What killed my friend were the grave emotional and mental disorders caused by growing up with parents who did not love themselves in a dysfunctional family in an emotionally-dishonest, Spiritually-hostile, shame-based society. What killed Robert was his Codependence. His relationship with himself was full of self-hatred and shame and he couldn't stay sober long enough to get to the point where he could deal with his childhood issues.

Robert was born with a genetic predisposition to have a fatal disease, Alcoholism. His childhood inflicted a second fatal disease on him. My friend Robert was one more of the many Alcoholics to die of codependency.

The Death of My Alcoholic Daughter

George McGovern

In the following excerpt from Terry: My Daughter's Life-and-Death Struggle with Alcoholism, *former senator and presidential candidate George McGovern tells of the night that he learned that his daughter Terry was found dead, frozen in the snow while intoxicated. He describes having to break the news to his wife and children, and details his final encounters with his troubled daughter. He also chronicles her struggle with alcoholism, including periods of sobriety and a relapse that caused her to lose custody of her children. Reflecting on Terry's untimely death, McGovern ponders his daughter's depression, low self-esteem, and feelings of abandonment. McGovern served in the U.S. Senate from 1963 to 1980. He unsuccessfully ran against presidential incumbent Richard Nixon as the Democratic candidate in the 1972 election. As of 2007, he is serving as the United Nations Global Ambassador on World Hunger.*

Unexpected Visitors

Shortly before 11:30 P.M., December 13, 1994, the doorbell rang at our home in Northwest Washington. We live in a quiet, secluded neighborhood known as Forest Hills that adjoins Rock Creek Park. It is unusual for anyone to ring a doorbell at this hour; not expecting visitors, I was startled.

On this Tuesday night, Eleanor and I had enjoyed a pleasant evening at Otello's Restaurant just below Dupont Circle— about ten minutes from our home. The owner, who sometimes doubles at the piano for the entertainment of his patrons, had played a couple of request numbers for us—the old Beatles song "Hey Jude" and some selections from *My Fair Lady*. I was still humming these tunes when we arrived home.

Eleanor had gone upstairs and was in bed reading a novel. After playing the piano for a few minutes, I had gone into our second-floor living room, lit a small log in our fireplace, and begun scanning the current issue of *Harper's* magazine. Puzzling over the late-night ringing of the doorbell, I went downstairs to see who might be there. As I descended the last steps of the open stairway I could see two men through the glass on each side of the large front door. One appeared to be a police officer, the other a clergyman. My heart sank. Their grave, official appearance did not portend welcome news.

Terrible News

"Senator McGovern, we're sorry to come to your home so late," said the officer, "but we have some sad news we must relate to you. Your daughter, Teresa Jane McGovern, was found dead today in Madison, Wisconsin, apparently frozen in the snow while intoxicated."

"Oh no!" I cried.

Then I simply went numb. I could not weep, or think, or speak.

"The Dane County coroner in Madison has asked us to tell you that he is standing by and wishes you to call him no matter how late the hour," the officer said. "We're sorry to bring you such bad news."

Trying to console me, the clergyman placed a hand on my shoulder and said a few comforting words. I thanked the two men for their kindness and then walked into my darkened den and began pacing slowly around the room. Aware there was nothing more they could do, the men quietly left.

As soon as I could manage to speak, I telephoned the coroner in Madison, Ray Wosepka. He knew the Wisconsin members of my family—my daughter Susan and her husband,

Jim Rowen, formerly of Madison and in recent years residents of Milwaukee, where Jim works at the *Milwaukee Journal-Sentinel* and Susan at the University of Wisconsin. The coroner also knew Teresa well enough to know that she had suffered from a longtime drinking problem. He gave me the few details available about her death and explained that he would have more information after an autopsy had been performed the next day. I was incapable of asking more than a few faltering questions, so I thanked the coroner for his thoughtfulness, hung up, and began pacing again.

Informing His Wife

And then it dawned on me: I must go upstairs and tell Eleanor that our troubled daughter, whom she had loved, nurtured, and laughed and cried with for so many years, was now gone—frozen in the December snows of Wisconsin. How could I possibly announce to dear Eleanor anything so utterly devastating? Could she withstand the shock?

I stalled for perhaps fifteen minutes before informing Eleanor of Terry's death, first because it was such a painful task, and second because I harbored a desperate hope that the coroner might call and tell me that they had revived Terry, or that they had made a mistake in identifying the body. But finally I trudged up the stairs to our third-floor bedroom. Eleanor was sleeping soundly—her reading lamp still lighted, her book fallen to the floor. As I looked at the lovely, gentle face on the pillow, I began to weep convulsively.

Gathering Eleanor in my arms as she awakened, I blurted out, "This is the saddest news I will ever tell you. Terry is gone. She died today in Madison, apparently after heavy drinking and a collapse in the snow." Eleanor's response was a cry heartrending and terrible. I can neither describe nor forget it.

"Oh God, oh God, what happened? What happened? No, no, no, no, no." All I could do was to hold her tightly and weep with her. It was the saddest moment of our more than fifty years of marriage.

As I tried to console Eleanor, I was seized by a searing pain that made me move away. Terry, the delightful but afflicted daughter I had been especially close to from the beginning, was dead. How could this be? How could this endearing child have drifted so far over the years that she ended up dying alone in the snow?

Pacing the floor, agonizing over these questions, I began to think of my other children. They must be told of Terry's death.

Terry's Siblings Are Told

It was shortly after midnight when I called our oldest daughter, Ann, a teacher in Riverdale, Maryland, and broke the news to her. Ann had expressed alarm for the past two years about Terry's deepening alcoholism. She and her husband, Frank Wilson, had even driven to Wisconsin in the spring of 1993 to be with Terry for a few days in what they feared might be her last months of life. Ann was stunned and grief-stricken to have her fears verified, but I sensed that it was in some way a confirmation rather than a total shock. She and her family arrived about two in the morning—it was then December 14—to be with us for the rest of the night. Meanwhile, I telephoned our second daughter, Susan, in Milwaukee. She had been with Terry frequently in recent years and had believed for a while that by showing her love for her sister, she could somehow redeem her from alcoholism. Terry had first moved to Wisconsin in 1976 when Susan invited her to come and live with her and her husband and their two young sons, Matthew and Sam. The death of her younger sister sent Sue into a deep grief that has continued.

Our youngest daughter, Mary, was expecting to give birth to a second child in a few months, so I did not telephone her until early the next morning. As a rising United Nations professional, she had been out of the country or working in New York City over the past decade and was not as close to Terry as Susan and Ann. She also carried a measure of both personal and occupational stress that had prompted her to avoid becoming too enmeshed in Terry's struggles.

Steve, Terry's only brother, who is three years her junior, was not reachable by telephone during the night. Ann and her son Tim told him of Terry's death the next morning. Stunned, he left a friend's apartment and walked slowly down Connecticut Avenue. "Curiously," he later said, "a kind of calming relief came over me as I thought, 'Finally, Terry is at peace.' I found myself smiling through the tears."

Terry with Her Family

During the last two weeks of the previous June, our family, including Teresa and her two little girls, Marian, nine, and Colleen, seven, had gathered for a vacation in a big house on North Carolina's Outer Banks. Ann and Susan were there with their husbands and five sons, along with Eleanor and me. Terry, an accomplished swimmer, loved the ocean. We all enjoyed the sun, surf, and saltwater spray on the vast beaches of the Atlantic, although Terry struggled at times against her craving for alcohol. She could not always hide her pain; her normal enthusiasm and cheerfulness were somewhat subdued during these days.

Terry's brother-in-law, Jim Rowen, recalls a moment when he and Terry found themselves relaxing on the sand while the children splashed in the ocean. Aware of the tension that sometimes existed in the family because of her drinking, Terry tried to break the ice by asking Jim how he thought the Milwaukee Brewers baseball team would fare that season. "She knew I was a baseball nut, but I knew she didn't give a damn about professional sports, yet she wanted to embrace me conversationally by coming over on my ground," Jim noted.

When asked to recall pleasurable moments with their mother, Marian and Colleen talked excitedly about Terry's twice taking them to a popular carnival on the Outer Banks complete with rides on the roller coaster. They remember

Terry's smiling face as she waved to them on their rides, obviously relishing their fun. But they also recall their mother's embarrassment and apology when they discovered that she had downed a large bottle of ale.

Terry lived with this kind of dichotomy for most of her life: a fun-loving, humorous, engaging personality who brought joy to her family and friends—but also, at times, the clouds of alcoholism and depression.

Terry Made People Laugh

Her wit and infectious laughter have been noted by every one of her friends I have interviewed. Dawn Newsome, who knew her intimately over many years, tells of Terry's "earthy" sense of humor, which she witnessed on a shopping mission when Terry was interested in buying a pair of Timberland boots. "Why are they so much more expensive than the other brands? Are they worth the difference?" Terry asked the clerk. Very seriously, the clerk inquired, "Do you really want me to give you all the facts?" "Naw," said Terry, "just give me a crock of shit." The somber clerk burst out laughing.

"I can't recall once when Terry failed to come up with a quip when she needed a retort to bring down the barriers," Dawn told me. "No matter how young or old, mighty or humble, Terry sooner or later would have people laughing, or at least feeling better."

The Last Contact with Terry

There are times in the alcoholic's life, however, when humor fails—seemingly every cell in the body screams in real pain for alcohol. Those terrible times were never far from closing in on Terry. The nonalcoholic cannot grasp the genuine anguish involved. Terry did not escape that distress on the Outer Banks, but largely she resisted it with a supreme effort to protect the pleasure of the rest of us. That was the last time we saw her alive.

Following that family vacation, Eleanor and I took off for the University of Innsbruck, Austria, where I was a guest lecturer for the next six weeks. Terry returned to Madison with her daughters. We had very little contact with her during the summer and early fall. Indeed, we had decided—with the encouragement of a counselor—that it might be best for both Terry and for us not to be deeply involved for a time.

In mid-November, Eleanor and I left Washington on a business trip to the Persian Gulf, ending with a few days in Italy and a Thanksgiving dinner at the lovely mountain seaside home of our friend Gore Vidal. Just before that trip, Eleanor received a letter from Terry postmarked November 4 in which she wrote:

> *I truly cannot believe I've let myself stay sick for so long. It's been 4 years relapsing—pulling my life apart and damaging the spirits of those I love most. I wonder if I can ever really have a full life knowing my children and I have lost precious time and not knowing what time I will be allowed now. I'm so sad mom. Please pray for Marian, Colleen and me to be reunited. I want to be a daughter to you and dad—not a source of worry, anger and sorrow. I want to be a sister to my brother and sisters. I've played around with my recovery—somehow unable to grasp how serious it is, how much suffering it has caused me and others.*

We had only a few brief telephone conversations with Terry during the next few weeks, hoping that our maintaining a certain distance might prompt her to confront her alcohol dependence. But her drinking problem steadily worsened during this period from mid-July to mid-December.

There has not been a day since Terry's death that I have not anguished over our decision. I regret every phone call not made, every letter not written, every missed opportunity to be with her and to share her pain.

Terry's Period of Sobriety

From October 1980 until the summer of 1988, Terry maintained the longest period of sobriety in her adult life. It was during this period that she met and fell in love with Raymond Frey, a Wisconsin social worker. Although they never married, they lived together for several years and became excellent parents to two daughters, Marian, born in 1985, and Colleen, born in 1987. They faced the usual strains and pressures of trying to rear children and maintain a home on a limited income, but they also developed clashing emotional needs that made it difficult to sustain their relationship. Terry, a recovering alcoholic, was also a sensitive and loving person who desperately needed the emotional support of an affectionate and caring mate. Ray was caught up, as are so many young fathers, in making a living. He perhaps needed more personal distance than Terry could tolerate. After five years of living together, they came to a mutual agreement that Ray should leave, at least for a trial period. Terry believed that after a few weeks of separation, Ray would miss her as much as she did him, and would return as a more understanding and loving mate. But this was not to be.

Ray had scarcely departed in mid-October 1988 before Terry went into a painful time of alternating regret, jealousy, resentment, sorrow, anger, and self-pity, culminating in her relapse into drinking. She lacked the personal resources to care for two energetic, demanding little girls by herself; nor could she escape the sense of rejection she felt because Ray had begun a new relationship with a woman who had also been Terry's friend.

Terry Enters a Recovery Program

When an alcoholic relapses after a lengthy sobriety, recovery is extremely difficult. The disease continues its insidious course even in sobriety and grips the victim with new force when a relapse occurs. To her credit, Terry recognized the seriousness of her resumed drinking and placed herself in a long-term recovery program in Milwaukee. A young mother invariably finds such a program especially painful and difficult because it separates her from her dependent children. But Terry succeeded over the next year with a determined effort.

Four days into this experience at Recovery House, she wrote in her journal on October 29, 1989:

Sitting here in my room, feeling the old, familiar gnawing emptiness, I know I must continue with my meditation. It is the most valuable time I have. . . . I listen to the wind. I wish I were in my new home listening to this wind while my babies sleep.

But at the end of the day, she knew that she must remain in Milwaukee struggling with her recovery:

11:15 p.m. The day is over and I'm going to bed with a good feeling. What I learned today that will help me stay sober are some of the things that caused my relapse:

1. *I didn't want to give up drinking completely—*
2. *Dishonest—if I had been honest I would have thought through the consequences. I didn't because I was in DE-NIAL.*
3. *Tried to do it alone—thought therapy and self knowledge were my best tools—*
4. *Didn't develop my spiritual life*
5. *Stopped going to meetings [AA]*
6. *Stopped using a sponsor.*

Here I will learn the attitudes and thought patterns that lead to unhappiness and then using.

This energetic, full-time recovery program meant that for the first time Ray was the primary caretaker of four-year-old Marian and two-year-old Colleen. He cooperated in driving the children from Madison to Milwaukee for a visit each weekend. Terry's treatment continued for much of 1990 as she received outpatient care while living in her own apartment in Milwaukee. All went well until she decided to move back to Madison to be with her children. Then the same old anxieties, stresses, and depression returned, and she sought relief in her old friend alcohol. She made other serious efforts in recovery programs in Wisconsin, Washington, D.C., and Maryland— but each in turn was soon followed by a relapse.

Terry's Many Relapses

During the last four years of her life—beginning March 25, 1991, and ending December 12, 1994—she was admitted to the Tellurian Detox Center in Madison sixty-eight times— usually after collapsing and sometimes injuring herself while heavily intoxicated. On one occasion, she fell facedown in a pool of water and nearly drowned. Several times she suffered painful head or facial abrasions from falling on the sidewalks or streets of Madison. At other times, she passed out on a bus, on a park bench, or in a store and was then taken to the detox center or a nearby hospital after someone called 911. She became a familiar, forlorn figure to the Madison police, emergency crews, and hospitals and the ever-beckoning detox center.

Life in Detox

These many detoxifications kept Terry alive, but they were miserable experiences. One veteran of such places describes it this way: "Imagine yourself withdrawing from alcohol in a detox ward. You may be racked with tremors so severe you can't lift a cup of coffee. Your stomach feels like it wants to leap up your throat. Every muscle in your body aches. You can hardly walk to the bathroom."

Laura Blumenfeld, a *Washington Post* reporter who wrote of Terry's death in the Sunday, February 5, 1995, issue, has captured some of the conditions Terry lived with as she moved in and out of the Tellurian Detox Center in her last months:

As the months passed, her stomach swelled, the veins in her esophagus dilated, and she was throwing up blood. . . . In the spitting, cursing, dark halls of detox, where alarms blare if patients break the laser beams across their doors, where the cinder-block walls are covered with squares of foam so patients don't crack their heads, Terry was something of an oddity. She believed she would get well. She was sweet and articulate. She read books and used Estée Lauder blush.

There was another difference with Terry. She was one of the only patients who still had people on the outside who cared. Her father was always sending her roses. When the roses withered, she wound them around her headband, smiling: "They love me, they do."

Even at the detox center, while her body jittered from withdrawal, she would limp out of bed to soothe her roommate, or pad down the hall in a robe to bring her orange juice. In group therapy she liked to comfort others, rather than focus on her own troubles.

Her warmth helped heal other alcoholics even if she couldn't heal herself. One friend from detox, a man named Don, tells of the time he escaped from a treatment facility with a lunatic plan to run away to Bangkok. He called Terry from the platform at the Amtrak station. She had precisely fifteen minutes to persuade him to come back to the facility.

Later, they celebrated his sobriety by spray-painting his initials on a rock along with his recovery date, 12/25/89. Christmas. Then Don sprayed TJM. Teresa Jane McGovern. He asked her, "What's the anniversary of your recovery?"

She smiled crookedly and said: "Just put a question mark."

In early 1993, in an effort to break this increasingly sad and dangerous pattern, Eleanor and I persuaded Terry to enter a special treatment program at the National Institutes of Health in Bethesda, Maryland. She cooperated, as did Eleanor and I, with the six-week treatment agenda, which included counseling and group-discussion sessions with family members of other patients. We were encouraged by Terry's serious effort, hopeful attitude, and apparent progress into recovery.

Unable to Stop Drinking

On the morning of her completion of the program, I drove to the NIH center and brought her to our Washington home. She asked if she could use my car for a few minutes to pick up a prescription at a nearby drugstore. Three hours later I was called by a concerned bartender who informed me that Terry had collapsed from heavy drinking. It pains me even now to recall the sad and bitter disappointment, the personal regret and doubt about my own judgment, that followed. And let me be frank about this. I was furious. How many times should we arrange these treatment programs for her? How many thousands of dollars should we invest in failing efforts to assist her recovery? What about the resentment of our other children, who felt that their parents were obsessed with Terry?

"I guess the best way to get attention in this family is to be an alcoholic," Ann once told me.

Were we helping Terry, or enabling her to put off facing her addiction and coming to grips with it? Perhaps indirectly we were contributing to an illness that, if not confronted, could claim her life.

"Dad, I don't think Terry will ever get well as long as you and Mom keep bailing her out," my daughter Susan told me with a mixture of disgust and anguish.

A few months later, while having lunch with Michael Deaver, a longtime aide to President Reagan, I mentioned my deep concern over Terry's drinking problem. He immediately arranged for her to go through one of the most highly regarded treatment centers in the nation—Father Martin's Ashley House at Havre de Grace, Maryland. Michael drove her there himself that same night, after picking her up at Georgetown University Hospital.

After six weeks of a specialized program designed to pre-
pare patients against the danger of future relapses, Terry was
urged to live for the next six months or more in the supportive environment of a halfway house with other recovering alcoholics. She, however, was desperate to return to Madison to
be with her daughters, so she rejected this advice, as she had
on earlier occasions. Eleanor agreed to accompany her to
Madison and remain until she could find an apartment and a
job. With her usual patience and love, Eleanor stayed with her
for two weeks, but the day she left, Terry started drinking
again.

"How can you keep doing this to yourself and to your
family?" I asked.

"I don't know, Dad," she said wearily. "I guess I'm just an
alcoholic."

The Struggle for Sobriety

And yet, never once did Terry give up the struggle to move
from relapses back to sobriety. With her body crying out in
pain for alcohol, her spirit longed for sobriety. Physically she
got high temporarily on alcohol and then crashed into despair
again. But the high her heart and mind craved was simply to
feel stable and secure. All the evidence and the testimony of
her closest friends leave no doubt that Terry tried until the
end to resist the powerful claims of her body against her spiritual longing for a sober, satisfying life. Her sister Susan has
noted that Terry's journals tell of a valiant and perceptive nur-
turing of her soul even while her body was falling victim to
alcoholism.

Her diary of 1993 carries these poignant notations: "August 25: Last Drink. August 26: First day sober"—with a colorful X. Each day thereafter is highlighted by a Magic Marker
X indicating a day of sobriety until September 14, when the
notation reads, "Relapse"—with no X. The next day, September 15, she simply notes, "crying"—but with an X indicating

she stayed sober despite her misery. The "crying" appears again the next day with another sobriety X. Two more X's appear on September 17 and 18, and then no more—nineteen days of sobriety, a one-day relapse, four more days of painful sobriety, and then a relapse. This was the pattern of much of the last four years of her life, except for longer periods of abstinence when she was confined for treatment, and increasingly shorter times of nondrinking and more frequent relapses when she was not confined.

Abandonment, Low Self-Esteem, and Depression

As I have pursued the course of Terry's life since her death and pulled my own recollections into at least some degree of coherence, I am convinced that she was haunted by a growing sense of abandonment, a loss of self-esteem, and a painful, recurring depression. Those feelings were strongly fed by the departure of Ray. They were also aggravated by the ending of subsequent relationships, including one of special significance a year before her own death. A young male friend and sometimes drinking partner of Terry's named Steve, whom she cared for deeply and whose companionship she treasured, died alone, intoxicated, in the snow only a couple of blocks from Terry's eventual place of death. Terry brooded constantly over this loss, which led to many hours of sorrow, regret, and loneliness. She and Steve had talked about working together on their recovery and then marrying. She had once asked Eleanor and me to accompany her to the place of Steve's death, where we each placed a flower as she said yet another farewell to her fallen friend. The pattern of her death so closely duplicated Steve's that it is possible his death provided a blueprint for her own.

On July 29, 1990, ten months after her separation from Ray, this notation appears in her journal:

Abandonment—I feel it—it hurts. No one to make me feel safe, protected. I cry. . . . I have looked so long for someone to protect me, love me without anger or shame. I feel anxious, hold my breath. If someone looks too closely, I freeze like a chameleon—ready to change color (identity) to protect myself. Better to freeze.

—who can hurt me when I'm frozen?

Terry Loses Her Children

Behind the sense of abandonment and loss of self-esteem was the ever-lurking alcoholism that frequently separated her from friends, recreation, romance, social acceptance, and even the treasures of her life—her two little daughters. When Ray was given primary custody of her children, a vital part of her reason for being died. She sought constantly to offset these losses by telephone calls and socializing with a wide circle of friends who loved her and delighted in her company—when she was sober; they were never quite certain when alcohol might interrupt the relationship. She spent many long days and nights alone, except for a kitten, parakeet, dog, turtle, or some other pet, sometimes in apartments that she would rent for a while and then lose, or in the spare bedroom of a friend's home.

She treasured her shabby, secondhand furniture, her pictures and other wall hangings, her jewelry, her carefully preserved journals, photo albums, letters, and gifts, and the drawings and papers her children brought home from school. Each time she lost an apartment, she would carefully load all of her things into a small truck—sometimes borrowed from a friend—and place everything back in storage. No matter how ill she became, no matter how discouraged with her life, she clung to these personal treasures to the end. It has astounded me, as I have gone through her possessions, to discover how this desperately ill daughter preserved everything, going back in some cases to the early years of her life. I think she must have protected every little trinket ever given to her.

Terry's Alcoholism Worsens

Separated from her possessions as she frequently was, she felt deserted and homeless. Her medication of choice for these sad times was alcohol. As her brain cells were more and more impaired with alcohol, she was increasingly unable to control either her intake or her decision-making capability. In the last year of her life, she told her sister Ann, "My body no longer recognizes any food other than alcohol." Its ravages steadily made everything in her life worse. But as the disease progressed, she tried to protect us from anxiety by withholding information about her deepening illness.

I fear that we unwittingly added to her sense of abandonment by following the advice to distance ourselves in the last months of her life when she may have most needed to feel our love and presence. She called a friend, Don Berlin, collect from a pay phone, having just been released from the detox center shortly after Thanksgiving—two weeks before her death. Eleanor and I were traveling in the Middle East, and Terry was aware that we had stepped back somewhat from involvement with her. She also tended to hold me responsible for the "distancing" in the last months of her life. "I understand why they are doing it," she told Don, "but I feel bad about it. I only wish that my dad knew how much I love him."

I wish I could tell her: "Dear Terry, I hope you know how much I love you. And I wish I had told you that more when you were alive and struggling with the demon that controlled your brain." I try not to berate myself for the things that I cannot now correct, but if I had those months to live over again. . . .

"Alcoholism Is a Disease"

Well, I will tell you what I would do with a second chance: I would never forget that alcoholism is a disease, that I should hate the disease but care for its victim—just as I would react if a loved one were suffering from cancer or diabetes. I tried to maintain these attitudes with Terry, but frequently my anger at her behavior in the grip of alcoholism translated into resentment and disappointment directed at her instead of her illness.

Sometimes when I called her I would begin: "Who's ahead today—you or the demon?" She loved that way of posing the problem. It was a clear indication that I was separating the demon that I hated from the precious victim whom I loved.

But there should have been more of this understanding, and it should have been given more force and consistency. Terry, as a desperately ill human being suffering from alcoholism, should not have been left to walk and fall in the streets, to be evicted from her apartments, to drink herself into a state of blackout and collapse in public bars, to be exploited sexually and abused by strangers when she was intoxicated. She needed the unbroken love, support, and protection of her family, her friends, her neighborhood, and her community.

Alcoholics Need Love, Compassion, and Understanding

I ask God and I ask dear Terry to forgive me for not always faithfully adhering to these simple concerns as a father and as a member of the human family. There is no such thing as too much compassion, understanding, support, and love for the sick and dying. Alcoholics are sick unto death. They won't make it through the night without our love and protection—and sometimes our repeated direct intervention.

It is not easy to live with alcoholics, but it is far harder to live without them when death steals them away. I do not regret one single act of kindness, patience, or support that I gave to Terry. What I regret is her slowly developing death and the feeling that I could have done more to prevent it.

Nor can I escape regret over the ways in which my political career and personal ego demands deprived Terry and my other children of time, attention, direction—and fun with their father. This was a loss to me as much as to them. Almost from the beginning, there was a special relationship between Terry and me. After dubbing her "the Bear," sometimes I would attach her teddy bear to a string on the light over her bed and would awaken her for school by tapping lightly on her nose. She would smile sleepily and open her eyes knowing my trademark wake-up call.

We thrived on a shared sense of humor, a penchant for kidding, a sense of the ridiculous. She treasured that relationship, and, as the middle child separated by several years in age from her two older sisters and her younger brother and sister, she needed it.

It is sad for me to read passages in her personal journal describing the hurt and sense of loss she experienced as her dad became more and more caught up in public concerns and his personal gratification while having less and less time for her private needs. My other children have, I suppose, made similar notations. Daughters especially need a responsive and caring relationship with their fathers during adolescence. I am only comforted by the knowledge that in the fifteen years since I left the U.S. Senate, I have enjoyed much more time of close association with my children and grandchildren.

I am now certain that alcoholism is in considerable part a physiological disease based on the victim's genetic inheritance. It is probably arrogant for me to assume, as I sometimes have, that I had the power to prevent or cure that disease in one of my children. Terry drank too much—not because of anything she or Eleanor or I did or did not do, nor because she lacked willpower. She drank too much because she was an alcoholic. Her first drinks as an early teenager seem to have been stimulated by peer pressure; her later addiction stemmed at least in part from a genetic vulnerability that accompanied her at birth. As the saying goes among alcoholics, "One drink is too much, a thousand too little."

My son, Steve, a recovering alcoholic, sheds some light on the cravings of alcoholics in an interview with Laura Blumenfeld:

"I can numb the pain," says a voice. "It doesn't sound like an evil voice. It sounds like a friend, telling you the truth."

Teresa's younger brother, Steven McGovern, is describing the voice of alcohol, as it whispers to you when you are feeling tense or dissatisfied or empty: "Here's your old pal, I can get you through this." . . .

"At first," says Steve, "it sounds like the solution to all your vague unnamed fears. Then the fog clears. And the voice is laughing at you.

"'Gotcha again.'"

"You're left standing alone, among the destruction. You realize it took twenty years of your life. You're sober, you feel itchy, shaky, your chest squeezes and it's hard to breathe. Your body is crying for it."

The night Steve heard of Terry's death, he lay in bed and smiled, and he talked to his sister:

"Well, you're free now!"

"I couldn't help feeling happy for her. We were celebrating together. We were laughing and hugging."

The Week Before Terry Died

On December 7, one week before her death, Terry called me at 9:45 A.M. to ask if I could help her with the financing of an apartment, which I agreed to do. She then left the detox center, ending a five-day confinement, and made her way to the Marquette Elementary School in time for an 11:15 lunch with Marian. She loved brief times such as these with her daughters, who were the joys of her life. Marian and Colleen savored such visits with their mother too, but they became increasingly anxious when Terry appeared after she had been drinking.

Records at the detox center for the previous three weeks tell a story: Terry was admitted November 14 and discharged later the next day, and then readmitted the same day, discharged November 17 and readmitted the same day, discharged November 19, readmitted November 20, discharged November 22, readmitted November 23, left of her own volition November 29, readmitted December 1, left of her own volition December 2, and readmitted the same day. After being released December 7, she remained sober until after her lunch with Marian shortly before noon.

But during the afternoon the drinking resumed, and by the time she visited seven-year-old Colleen's Lapham Elementary School she was partially intoxicated. She arrived at 3:00 P.M. when Colleen was just getting on the school bus to go home. Terry joined her on the bus, quietly apologizing for her drinking. "Mommy, I wish you didn't drink, but I want to be with you whether you're drinking or not," Colleen said. Terry said goodbye to little Colleen on the porch of her home on Rutledge Street. It was the last time she was to see either of her daughters.

Terry's First Collapse in the Snow

At eight o'clock that night, she stumbled into a familiar cooperative grocery store in her old neighborhood on Williamson Street, not only intoxicated but also wet and cold from an apparent earlier collapse in the heavy snow.

Anna Bose, a clerk in the store, where Terry had shopped over the years, noted that her late-evening visitor was shaking from the cold; she was probably suffering from frostbite and hypothermia. She was also finding it difficult to speak with any coherence. After calling 911 for an ambulance, Anna asked

Terry to sit with her, comforted her, and began rubbing her hands and feet with dry towels.

"And we both cried," she wrote us. "I told her that she was doing just fine, and she responded to the contact and the kindness. She kissed me on the cheek and said, 'I know you.' And I thought—I know you and how you are struggling."

Later that night after the paramedics had taken her to St. Mary's Hospital for treatment, an orderly went into the examination room to check on her. He found her curled up in a ball under a blanket, soaking wet, shivering and frightened, it was not the first time he had encountered Terry at St. Mary's. Dropping to his knees, he asked: "Why are you doing this to yourself?"

Rocking in agony, she could only say: "I don't know. I don't know." And, indeed, she could never explain her cruel and punishing self-inflicted bouts with alcohol. Later that night, when her condition stabilized, she was taken back to the detox center, where she had been released earlier in the day.

The next afternoon, she called me at my office to ask again if I would help her secure a lease on an apartment near the house where her children lived with their father. She explained that she had saved $600 to cover the security deposit on the apartment but had lost it while drinking the night before. When I expressed my disappointment over her drinking and the loss of her money, she said: "Well, Dad, it could have been worse—I could have lost my life." I, of course, readily agreed, although I knew nothing of the close call in the snow the night before.

"Terry, your life is everything," I said. "I'll help you with the apartment, but please take care of yourself. We've sent roundtrip airline tickets for you and the little girls and we're looking forward to your being home for Christmas."

She assured me that all would be well—although I detected a slight anxiety in her voice about the flight home for

Christmas, a flight she knew she would be unable to make if the drinking resumed. In a call a few days earlier, she had asked me if I could determine whether her health coverage would pay for her admission to a long-term-care facility where she had once been a patient in suburban Milwaukee. What she did *not* tell me was that her counselors at the detox center had told her they were instituting steps to secure a court order that would place her involuntarily in a different long-term-care facility in Milwaukee. Although I did not know it at the time, she was terrified by this prospect and was determined to leave the detox center before such a court order could be secured and served. She had refused to sign a consent form that would authorize her counselors to give us this information or any other information about her condition. Some months earlier, in the summer, in a telephone conversation with her counselor, I had approved the committal plan with the understanding it would be followed only if it seemed to be the only option that might save her.

Terry Avoids Involuntary Care

Terry's first priority in her last days was to avoid involuntary long-term care. She could not bear the thought of another lengthy separation from her daughters, nor did she have much faith in the success of yet another program. That was doubtless her reason for asking me to find out if she could voluntarily return to the earlier treatment center, where she would be free to walk away to see her daughters or to reach the nearest bar. Her counselors objected to the treatment center preferred by Terry in part because one of its attractions for her was a male patient there who had in the past complicated the recovery process for her. Her alternative plan of securing an apartment was also, I now know, a strategy for avoiding the serving of a court order at the detox center. This type of scheming is typical self-destructive alcoholic behavior—maddening for caring friends, counselors, and family members. It's the product of a brain long affected by alcohol.

In and Out of Detox

Shortly after Labor Day, Terry had accepted an invitation from a longtime friend, Art Lahey of nearby Horicon, Wisconsin, to stay for a while at his home, where he resided with his son. His wife, a close friend of Terry's, had died early in 1994. Terry remained sober during September and early October— even while working part-time as a waitress at a Horicon café. When her drinking resumed, Art took her back to the detox center, but stayed in frequent contact with her while she was there from October 10 until October 24, at which point she transferred to the Madison Hope Haven halfway house, where she remained until November 13. Then began the series of admissions and discharges at the detox center, which continued until her death a month later.

She was at Hope Haven on Halloween, which she wanted to be memorable for her two young daughters. She carefully worked out with them the costumes they wanted to wear: for Marian, the garb of a nun, and for Colleen, Snow White. Under Terry's instructions, Eleanor devised a child-sized nun costume and mailed it to Marian. Terry was unable to attend the Halloween party, but she proudly mailed us pictures of the girls with her at Hope Haven on the day before Halloween and other shots of the girls in their Halloween gowns.

Art had informed Terry that although it was painful for him, he had agreed to testify in court, as requested by the detox counselors, that she was unable to care for herself. Terry was dismayed. She begged him not to do so, and he finally agreed to withhold his testimony if Terry was able to stop drinking after going forward with the leasing of her apartment.

Terry Secures a New Apartment

Thus fortified, she made an appointment to see her prospective landlord at the new apartment at 2:00 P.M. on Monday,

December 12. Early that morning, as she had requested, I assured her landlord that I would guarantee the rent should she be unable to pay it.

Then, against the wishes of her counselor, she left the center and headed for a 10:00 A.M. appointment with an old friend, Ernie Moll. He had several years earlier helped her and her children after her separation from Raymond Frey. At one time, Ernie had even constructed a little house for the girls' pet mice. Terry had telephoned him on December 7, telling him she was worried about possible involuntary commitment to long-term treatment and asking him to help her move into an apartment. She called again on December 9 to ask if he would go to her mailbox at her apartment to see if an expected check from Eleanor was there. The check was there, and Ernie promised to hold it for her until their meeting on December 12. She arrived promptly at 10:00 A.M. on the 12th and seemed to be in high spirits.

She and Ernie spent a pleasant hour or so at his apartment, recalling good times of earlier years. Terry was excited about her new home and was pleased that her friend offered her an air mattress and a chair for temporary use and presented her with a carefully wrapped package containing her three photo albums, which he had stored for her for several years. He also agreed to build another mouse house as requested by nine-year-old Marian, provided she would help him.

Over a second cup of coffee, Ernie called a tenant in the apartment above his and arranged to borrow his pickup truck so that Terry's furniture and personal effects in storage could be moved to the new apartment on Wednesday, December 14, sometime after 5:00 P.M. "I thought this might be the attempt that works. She seemed so clear and upbeat about things," Ernie later wrote us.

Having lost her personal identification cards, including her driver's license, along with her money in the incident of December 7, Terry was worried that she would have difficulty cashing a check. Loading her albums and other personal things into his car, Ernie drove her to the Department of Motor Vehicles office to get a new driving permit, for which he provided the necessary $4. Remembering that she had lost her glasses in the earlier collapse, Ernie helped her fill out the application and then walked with her to the photo department. Always conscious of her appearance, which by her lights required modestly applied lipstick and appropriate earrings, Terry jokingly asked her friend if he had any lipstick. Even without those benefits, she proudly showed off the new instant photo, in which she wore a broad smile. In his letter to us of Thursday, December 15, Ernie wrote:

> As we left the building, Terry stopped to offer assistance to an elderly man on crutches, who seemed to be having quite a struggle navigating the ice and snow at the curb. He said he was doing okay, but she took his arm anyhow to steady him as he hobbled into the building. I went ahead to the car, unlocked the doors, and got in. When she had completed her helpful task, we drove back to her apartment on Morrison Court to unload the items from the car. We were able between us to take all of the things up to the third-floor apartment in one trip. We arrived there to find two of the workmen who had done the remodeling. The floors were fleshly sanded and varnished. The kitchen was all new, cupboards, appliances, and work counter, all new. A very nice apartment, with a view over the trees and rooftops toward Lake Monona. Plenty of room for the children to visit and stay over, if that was an option. Terry talked with the men about the appointment with the landlord at 2:00 p.m. They told her the place was all ready except for cleaning and carpeting in one room. They gave her a key.

> I returned to the car to move it out of the driveway, where it blocked the way for other tenants. Terry came down a few minutes later. By this time it was about 12:15 p.m. Terry was confident she could go to the bank, cash the check, and re-

turn in time for the appointment. She said she had several bus passes. I assumed she would take a bus on Williamson, back to the neighborhood, and walk the few blocks over to Morrison Court. I drove to her bank across from the main library on West Main and left her there. I went to a restaurant, had lunch, and returned home.

I had expected her to call me on Tuesday or Wednesday to give me information about getting the basic items from storage. I didn't hear from her on Tuesday but was only slightly concerned. . . . On Wednesday morning, a friend called to tell me they had found her.

After cashing her check, Terry returned to the apartment in time for her 2:00 P.M. meeting with her new landlord, Bob. She had given him a $500 security deposit in November and now turned over $550 from her just-cashed check for the first month's rent.

Bob, about to observe his sixty-seventh birthday, was himself a recovering alcoholic and sympathetic to Terry. They spent the next three hours visiting and turning the pages of the photo albums that spanned her life. She told Bob of her love for her mother and father, her brother and sisters, and her little girls. She spoke excitedly about her new apartment and how wonderful it would be to have this comfortable home with a lake view located within a block of Marian and Colleen. About 5:00 P.M., as her landlord prepared to leave, she put her hands on his shoulders and said affectionately, "You know, Bob, you remind me of my father. You're very compassionate."

After agreeing to meet her landlord at the apartment again the next day at 1:00 P.M. to take care of a few minor unfinished modifications, Terry said good night, noting that she had to walk over to nearby Williamson Street to pick up a few items for the apartment. As evening approached, a damp, chilling fog crept across the city and the temperature dropped far below freezing.

Terry Was Dressed for the Cold

Terry was warmly and neatly dressed, wearing thermal underwear, dark slacks, a heavy off-white Sandhills (N.C.) Community College pullover shirt I had given her, a red-and-black winter jacket, and a warm woolen scarf. She walked up Baldwin for three and a half blocks, crossing familiar streets where she had lived for the past seventeen years, including Rutledge, where Colleen and Marian lived with their father. I have no doubt that she walked the few paces to the left from Baldwin past the Rutledge house in the hope that she might catch a glimpse of her children through the window. She did this frequently—sometimes when she was weaving and stumbling from too much vodka. Returning to Baldwin, she would next come to Spaight, then Jenifer, where in earlier years she had rented apartments, and then her familiar neighborhood shopping street, Williamson.

Terry Begins to Drink

When Terry entered the Crystal Corner Bar at the intersection of Williamson and Baldwin shortly after 5:00 P.M., she took a stool at the forward end of the bar near the entrance. She struck up a conversation with a veteran of the Vietnam War, who bought her a vodka on the rocks. She chatted happily with other patrons about her new apartment and ordered another vodka and another. When the veteran invited her to have a drink with him at his apartment, she declined. She then asked him if he would like to see her new apartment, and he declined. My guess is that, knowing she was becoming intoxicated, she wanted someone to accompany her in the cold and darkness to her new home lest she fall or lose her way. At about 7:00 P.M., she telephoned her friend Kate, whose apartment Terry had been sharing during the brief intervals when she was not in detox. Detecting that Terry had been drinking, Kate tried to find out where she was so that she could come and bring her home. Kate had earlier assured

Terry that she would serve as her sponsor in the Alcoholics Anonymous recovery program, and would also be her landlord until she was ready for an apartment of her own.

Terry Continues to Drink

But Terry declined to say where she was, perhaps not wanting her sponsor and friend to see her intoxicated and also preferring to go to her own new apartment. She then left the Crystal Corner Bar, either of her own volition or at the request of the bartender, and walked up Williamson Street, perhaps to buy the items she needed at the Sunshine Market at the other end of the block. In any event, she stopped en route at Jamaica Jo Mama's Restaurant and Bar, where she ordered another drink. Shortly before 8:00 P.M., she left Jamaica Jo's, absentmindedly failing to pay her check, which was then taken care of by a patron who had been sitting next to her. Turning into an open area adjoining the bar, she apparently fell into a snowbank. After getting up, covered with snow, she entered without knocking the back door of the house next to the bar.

Frederika Armson, a young single mother, was working in her kitchen when Terry quietly walked into her living room, where her two little children were chatting on the sofa. Jennifer Sandecke, another young woman who shared the small house, was also in the living room watching television. Frederika had been expecting her mother and assumed that the person who had walked into her house unannounced was she. After a brief pause, she went into the living room and found Jennifer and the children looking puzzled and trying to engage the unknown intruder in conversation.

Terry Falls into Alcoholic Blackout

Terry seemed unable to speak but stood quietly smiling at the children, who were about the same ages as her own daughters. Frederika and Jennifer asked Terry if she had been injured in an accident or if she was on medication, but she remained silent, continuing to smile affectionately at the children. Based on her previous history, it appears Terry was in an alcoholic blackout.

Frederika, who later described the stranger as "well groomed, gentle, and unthreatening," nonetheless ordered her children to go upstairs while she went to the phone to call 911. But as she conferred with the police, Terry quietly slipped out of the house through the front door onto Williamson Street. Jennifer later noted that Terry seemed to know how to move quickly, unlock the door, and leave easily, "as though she were familiar with the house." Frederika followed Terry out past the next-door Lakeside Press building and then down a narrow driveway toward the rear of that building; there Terry veered off to the left behind the house on that side of the driveway. Frederika pointed out this route to the police team that arrived a few minutes later, but they were unable to find her.

About half an hour after leaving the Armson house, around 8:30 P.M., Terry was encountered by a neighbor, Doneva Cox. Ms. Cox was headed for the nearby Sunshine Market when she noticed Terry, apparently inebriated, standing at the Lakeside Press driveway entrance. She asked her if she was drunk, to which Terry replied, "Yes."

"Do you know where you live?" inquired Ms. Cox. Terry answered, "No."

Terry Returns to the Crystal Corner Bar

While the concerned woman watched, Terry walked slowly the fifty or so yards to the Crystal Corner Bar, where she had started the evening three hours earlier. She paused outside and then entered.

When I first talked to the manager by telephone several days later, he denied that anyone had seen Terry in his bar the night of her death. But when I arrived at the Crystal Corner unexpectedly a month later, two different bartenders talked rather nervously about her presence that night. Chris had served her after 5:00 P.M. until he went off duty at 7:00 P.M.; Todd, who began work at 7:00 P.M., said that Terry, after leaving the bar about then, returned obviously intoxicated at about 8:30 P.M. He said that he refused three times to serve her, prompting her to leave about five minutes after she arrived. No one claims to have seen her after she left the Crystal Corner Bar shortly after 8:30 P.M.

Police Look for Terry

Police Officer Sue Armagost and a Detective Gebler arrived at the Armson residence around 8:00 P.M. and were told that Terry had left the house walking west. They began searching that area on foot, which should have included the space behind the Lakeside Press next door to the Armson house. They also inquired about Terry at the Crystal Bar, but were given no information there. Meanwhile, Police Officer Chris Smith arrived at the Armson house and interviewed Frederika and Jennifer in more detail about the behavior of the woman who had entered their house. They told Officer Smith that Terry "had snow all over her as if she had fallen, but she did not appear to be injured."

Officers Smith and Armagost then drove around the neighborhood before returning to the Armson home, at which point Smith searched on foot the area behind the buildings to the east of the house. It was during this search that the bartender at Jamaica Jo's told Smith of a woman fitting Terry's description who had left his bar earlier. Smith and Armagost also checked other bars, including Jolly Bob's, which was closed, and the Wisconsin Inn, where no one had seen a person fitting Terry's description. Why the police failed to find her in this little neighborhood where she had been a familiar figure for so many years remains a troubling mystery to me.

Terry Is Found

At 12:45 in the afternoon the next day, Tuesday, December 13, an employee at the Lakeside Press, Jerrold Chernow, opened the back door of the shop to check whether there was space available for his car in the small parking area.

"Hey," he said, "there's a little kid passed out in the snow." The owner of the shop, Norman Stockwell, a slender bearded man (who as a teenager had distributed my campaign literature in the Wisconsin presidential primary of 1972, as had Chernow), went out to check on the fallen child.

"It's not a kid," Stockwell called out. "And whoever it is seems to be a lot more than just passed out. There's no pulse. Call 911," he shouted. Chernow phoned, but apparently did not hear all of Stockwell's observations; he told the 911 operator that he had found a child of approximately thirteen years of age without a pulse. *Washington Post* writer Laura Blumenfeld described the scene:

> The fingers were frozen hard. Her skin was colorless. Her socks had iced onto her feet. She lay next to a circle of footprints, a ring ten feet in diameter, her own sneakered prints tamped down upon each other, as if she had been trying to walk straight but could only make dizzy circles until she dropped.
>
> It was just after noon on December 13, raw and overcast in Madison, Wisconsin. In the minutes it took for the emergency crew to arrive, the printer ... knelt and covered the body with his coat.
>
> There's something about this woman, he thought. She had a delicate, poetic face. There was refinement to her, the dangling earrings, the russet hair smoothed into a barrette.
>
> She had no purse, no ID; she had fallen among garbage cans and dead sunflowers. Still, he was certain; this woman had a home.

Her gloves were missing, probably left in one of the bars. Her scarf had fallen to the ground in a car track eight or ten feet from her body. There was nothing in her pockets other than the key to her apartment and five $1 bills. She wore a wristwatch, two rings—one silver and one gold—and her beloved earrings. The 911 emergency crew, the police, and Deputy Coroner Philip Little, who examined Terry where she lay in the snow, quickly determined that she was dead. They had her body transported to St. Mary's Hospital, where she had been treated only six days earlier, and where an autopsy would be performed the next day at 2:00 P.M. They then reported to the news media that an unidentified woman had been found. Later that afternoon, two staff members at the detox center Terry had just checked out of the day before heard the report on the radio. Melody Music-Twilla and Gerry Kluever, counselors who had worked with Terry during her confinements at the center in recent years, suspected the unknown dead woman might be Terry. Melody telephoned the coroner's office about 5:30 P.M., and Little, the deputy coroner, who had photographed Terry's body at St. Mary's, suggested that he bring the pictures to the detox center for identification.

Half an hour later, Melody and Gerry gazed at the Polaroid and began to weep. There was Terry "looking as though she were simply sleeping"—the same vulnerable, delicate person who had left the center in high hopes only a few hours before.

Terry's Death

All indications are that after leaving the Crystal Corner Bar, Terry trudged the half block back to the print shop and walked into the driveway to the parking space just a few paces from the house she had entered thirty-five or forty minutes earlier. After wandering in a circle, she either lay down or fell into the snow, where bitter cold began asserting its claim. Doctors tell me that after initial chills and shivering she would soon begin to feel warm. Her body heat melted the seven inches of snow all the way down to the grass. But as the biting cold slowed her bodily functions, her heartbeat began to grow faint, and then it stopped. There was simply too much snow and cold fighting against too small a body, despite its tenacious and plucky heart.

Given the intense cold that night, Terry may have died before midnight of December 12, but since her body was not discovered until shortly after noon the next day, her death was officially recorded as of December 13. "Death due to hypothermia while in a state of extreme intoxication," according to the coroner's report.

Lingering Questions

I do not expect ever to read sadder words of finality. They force me to face so many questions about Terry's life and death. What could I have done differently? What if I had been a more concerned and actively involved parent when she was a little girl, or a fragile adolescent? Why wasn't I in closer touch with her in the final months? Knowing that alcoholism is a dangerous, often fatal disease, should I have intervened to have her committed indefinitely to a locked-door long-term-treatment facility?

More immediate questions also persist. Why couldn't the police find an intoxicated young woman wandering only a few steps from where the 911 call was made? Why did the bartenders and patrons at two bars let her go out alone into the subfreezing darkness obviously intoxicated?

Perhaps in the festive atmosphere of the Christmas season, people were thinking about their own pleasures and family concerns rather than the well-being of a stranger who was drinking too much. Perhaps others were a little high themselves from too many toasts to a merry Christmas. Perhaps there is an understandable tendency for people to avoid be-

coming involved with intoxicated people, who can behave un-
predictably and offensively. Perhaps it is unrealistic to expect
people to carry even momentarily the burdens of some other
person's drinking problem.

Of one fact I am certain: if Terry's role had been reversed
with some of the people who encountered her that night, she
would have done her best to guide the person in trouble on a
path to safety. Frederika Armson did her best in calling 911,
and she later told me that although Terry could not speak that
evening in her living room, Terry left her with a sense of having been "blessed" by her quiet and gently smiling presence.

Terry's Luck Finally Wore Out

When I expressed my concerns about these matters to an old
family friend well acquainted with Terry's unfailing compassion and sensitive nature, he responded: "George, in this tragedy, as in so much of our lives, the luck factor is often deci-
sive."

Terry had been lucky many times in her life—other people
had often come to her rescue when she was in trouble. Her
luck ran out in the cold of that Christmastide evening.

The luck factor is underscored by two actions on the part
of the two men at the print shop, Stockwell and Chernow.
Stockwell had left work at 6:30 P.M. on December 12 but returned around 8:45 P.M., parking his car on the street in front
of his shop. If he had used the parking area at the rear of his
shop, it is quite possible that he would have encountered
Terry either wandering in that space or lying in the snow
spotlighted by his headlights. If she had arrived later with his
car parked in that area, he would doubtless have discovered
her when he left work a second time late that evening.

Chernow, who had left work at 7:15 P.M. from the rear
parking area, is certain that Terry was not there at that time,
or he would have caught her in the beam of his headlights. In
the parking area, in addition to his car, were an old disabled

car belonging to Stockwell and a van belonging to someone at the University of Wisconsin. It was difficult for Chernow to maneuver in the snow past the van, so the next morning he parked his car on the street in front of the shop. It is unlikely that Terry was still alive that morning when Chernow arrived at work, but we cannot be sure. It was four hours later when he discovered her body while checking to see if the van had left, making room for him to move his car in from the street.

And there was a third piece of bad luck. A light on the rear of the building had been broken by mischievous youngsters a couple of nights earlier, leaving the parking area in darkness. Had the light been working, it would have illuminated the area the night of Terry's entrance, making it more likely that the searching police would find her, and if she was attempting to hide, she might not have considered this a safe hiding place.

"Living on Borrowed Time"

Of course, absent a successful intervention and recovery, Terry was living on borrowed time. The central question about her life and death does not turn on a failure of luck in the last hours of her life. The question is, how did a beautiful, endearing, quick-witted, compassionate, and perceptive little girl grow up to become an alcoholic powerless to control or save her life? Why wasn't she one of the fortunate ones who through medical diagnosis and the AA program are able to recover from the disease?

These questions have haunted me since that late-night ringing of my doorbell. If I have found even partial answers, it is because I have pursued Terry's story with a loving heart and a questioning mind over the forty-five years of her life. I must confess that while I loved and cherished this special daughter since she was a small child, it took her death, the amazingly consistent testimony of her friends, and her candid letters and journals to open my eyes fully to the fact that Teresa Jane

McGovern was all along one of the most lovable and loving human beings on this troubled earth. I do not believe that she needed to die. I regret terribly that she did. But perhaps in God's good time I shall come to see a redeeming purpose to this death in the snow.

SOCIAL ISSUES
FIRSTHAND

CHAPTER 4

Recovery

The Importance of a Support System for Addicts

The Advocate

In the following selection, the author shares the story of his addiction, tracing the process of developing a problem with alcohol, his attempts to quit, and his decision to accept help. He expresses his gratitude for his wife, children, mother, and friends, and the strong support network he has found. He also conveys his happiness and his appreciation for the positive changes that he has made in his life as a result of his recovery. The anonymous author is a member of Alcoholics Anonymous and The Lawyers Assistance Program, an independent organization that provides peer support and referral services to members of the legal community with substance abuse problems.

The Gradual Process of Becoming an Alcoholic

I grew up in a religious household with two parents who loved and cared for me. However, there were problems, and I found it difficult to accept, among other things, my parents' religious beliefs and rules. This led to rebellion in my teenage years and my first experiments with alcohol.

There is some debate as to whether some people are genetically predisposed to alcoholism. Whatever the merits of those arguments, I went into an alcoholic blackout during my first drinking experience. Despite that, I liked what alcohol did for me. I didn't become an alcoholic overnight. It was a gradual process, developed over the course of many years and throughout my law career.

As my career developed, so did my consumption of alcohol. At one time it was considered good manners to drink

The *Advocate*, "The Ongoing Process of Recovery and Personal Development: A Testimonial," vol. 61, May 2003. © 2002–2006, Vancouver Bar Association. Reproduced by permission of the publisher and author.

with the judge and opposing counsel while awaiting the jury's verdict. I believed in good manners and did a lot of drinking then, and almost any other time.

As the stress of handling trials increased, so did my drinking. What had once been considered good manners—such as drinking with the judge—now became a problem. Some nights are gone forever in a haze of alcohol and cigarettes. Where did alcohol take me? At the end I was in a coma in the hospital. I had a near-death experience, looking down on myself from above while my soul left my body—the type of experience that people are fond of writing books about. What I know of that experience is that I was dying and that I am lucky to be alive today.

Trying to Stop Drinking

I tried to stop drinking on my own, promising myself that I would have only two drinks a day, or that perhaps I would drink only beer, or only wine, and so on. I tried everything, but nothing worked. This was particularly disconcerting as I had been able to "take care" of everything else in life that I said I was going to do. If I said I was going to do it, I did it. If nothing else, I was stubborn. But being stubborn didn't work with alcohol. There are some humorous but paradoxical incidents, such as my memory of pouring vodka into my coffee after spending hours with a client and arranging help for his alcoholism and admittance to a treatment centre. Treatment centres, AA and other things could help my clients, but sitting around "talking" couldn't help me. I needed action, but what that "action" was I certainly didn't know.

Receiving Help from Others

In retrospect, this inability to stop myself without the help of others from drinking turned out to be my greatest blessing. It led me to the Lawyers Assistance Program and fellowships such as AA. At some point in my journey, I came to realize that sobering up was not the only issue. I believed that if I sobered up things would be "OK" in my life. What I came to realize was that alcohol masked and intensified certain problems and dissatisfactions with life. I had to deal with, and change, certain parts of my personality and outlook on life.

Happy to Be an Alcoholic

As a result of these life changes. I can say that I am happy to be an alcoholic. When I first heard somebody say this years ago, I thought, "You've got to be crazy! Who would want to be an alcoholic?" But it is a paradox worth accepting. Becoming an alcoholic forced me to make fundamental changes in my life. Without such fundamental changes, I was destined to go through life an unhappy person.

Change came to be a real part of my life. These changes have been good. I accept responsibility for who I was and what I did when I drank. In my drinking days, I blamed others and cried about the sad state of the world. People starving to death while Suharto makes off with 45 billion dollars was my rallying cry.

What I came to realize is that I can do little about the unfairness in the world at large. I can do a lot about changing myself. This change involved taking a real look at myself and putting real plans into action. Now, I run marathons. I am completing graduate school with a perfect grade point average. I have a wonderful relationship with my mother and tell her I love her every day. I have a wonderful family, with kids and a wife with whom I share an honest, loving and spiritual relationship. I have friends from all walks of life, including many lawyers around me. For example, when going through certain problems that resulted from my drinking, approximately 50 people from all parts of the community (including many lawyers) came forward to offer their support in very difficult circumstances.

Asking for and Accepting Help

These positive changes didn't happen overnight. They developed over years—years in which I constantly examined and accepted responsibility for my actions and myself. I learned to ask for help and to accept help that was offered. I also learned to care about and help others.

Does this mean that my life is perfect? Far from it. In fact, sometimes I can only get through life by looking back and remembering how terrible it was when I drank. I suffer from problems, such as depression. It is difficult for me to admit that I still have problems because admitting problems isn't valued highly in our society. But it is good to be honest in this article. I am working on my problems, and my life continues to get better. I am grateful to the Lawyers Assistance Program for the support I continue to get and for the opportunity to reach out and help others.

Grateful for a Strong Support Network

My depression doesn't seem to make sense as I am blessed with so much, such as the family and friends that I described earlier. I do know that without the Lawyers Assistance Program and AA I would be living a solitary, lonely life—if indeed I were alive at all. Without my family and their support, life would be difficult. I believe that I have been lucky in life—especially lucky that I have the Lawyers Assistance Program, my friends and family (including the lawyers that I work with) and AA and other groups that were there for me when I needed them.

A Physician Assistant's View of Alcoholics Anonymous

Mark Warnat

Mark Warnat presents his perspective on an Alcoholics Anonymous (AA) meeting that he recently attended as an observer. In the following selection, Warnat describes the meeting's open and welcoming environment, recording the stories told by the leader of the meeting and the other attendees. After remarking on how accepting the members are of one another despite differences in age, race, and social class, he concludes that Alcoholics Anonymous is a valuable resource and an important tool for health care professionals. Warnat graduated from the Northeastern University Physician Assistant program in 2005.

The Typical AA Meeting

The AA meeting was held in a stuffy basement filled with circa-1970s multicolored plastic chairs lined up in neat little rows in the middle of the floor. The fluorescent lighting and the color of the walls bathed everything in a yellow hue; everyone, including me, had a somewhat jaundiced appearance. It was a nonsmoking meeting, but the pungent aroma permeating the room made it obvious that many chain-smoking alcoholics have attended meetings in this basement. The function of the two tiny windows flanking the basement was suspect since they were not designed to open and they also did not provide much light. A coffeepot endlessly percolated in the background, and almost everyone in the basement was clutching a steaming foam cup.

The first thing that stood out is that no fewer than 40 people were attending this meeting—a meeting happening in

Mark Warnat, "One Day at a Time," *JAAPA: Journal of the American Academy of Physician Assistants*, vol. 18, January 2005. Copyright 2005 Advanstar Communications, Inc. Reproduced by permission of the publisher and the author.

the middle of the day, on a random Tuesday, in a midsize suburb of Boston. They appeared to represent a cross section of society. They were men and women, black and white, tall and short, fat and thin, young and old. Some wore suits, crisp white shirts, paisley ties, and silk vests. Some had dirt under their fingernails and torn jeans. Some looked like the stereotypical alcoholic—strung out, unkempt, constantly fidgeting, tapping their feet, shifting in their chairs. But others looked as calm and cool as the other side of the pillow, with everything seemingly under control.

At this point I came to my own sobering realization—the first of several I would have that day—that we all have the potential to become better healers if we can eliminate our own preconceived notions and prejudices about patients based on their outward appearance.

Paul's Story

This particular meeting, according to the booklet I received in the mail from Alcoholics Anonymous, was designated as an open speaker session. In the front of the room, behind a rickety metal desk, sat a middle-aged man wearing an Aeropostale sweatshirt and a baseball cap. His midsection was a bit pudgy, a striking contrast to the gaunt face.

Peering out from behind the curled brim of his cap, he began the meeting in the customary way: "Hi," he said. "I'm Paul, and I'm an alcoholic." The reply—"Hi, Paul!"—was quick and amplified from his one voice to our 40.

Paul started off by saying that he was nervous since this was the first time he had ever led a meeting. Paul's voice quivered, either from nerves or as a side effect of choking back the sadness that alcoholism had thrust upon his life. Probably it was from a bit of both. He told us how in 1999, after one of his usual drinking binges, he blacked out and lost an entire day. He described how from that day on, he battled the disease of alcoholism by attending up to six AA meetings a day.

He mentioned how much he needed these meetings because alcohol and drug abuse had alienated him from his family. He spoke of how much he missed his wife and children and how he hoped that, over time, they would be reintegrated into his newly established world of sobriety.

Throughout his gut-wrenching speech, Paul took full responsibility for his circumstances. He didn't blame anyone—not his wife, his children, his former boss, Sam Adams, Jose Cuervo, Captain Morgan, Osama Bin Laden, God, or the economy. He was contrite. He blamed himself, and he was trying his best to make amends for the wrongs he had done and to slay his personal demons.

Celebrating Sobriety

Paul talked for about 15 minutes before opening the floor to other attendees. Seven people used the remainder of the hour to tell their own stories. Each had an equally awful tale of how the bottle, the needle, or the pill case led to their downfall. Some finished their monologue on a happy note, speaking of redemption and blissful reunions. Others did not.

After the open forum came an announcement that the group would now give brightly colored poker chips to those who had been able to go a certain period of time without abusing. These chips were small trinkets to mark a milestone in sobriety. The chip itself was worth a fraction of a penny, yet what it represented was invaluable. "Nine months . . . nine months . . ." was yelled out. Two women walked to the front of the room and, sheepishly yet proudly, grabbed the little plastic representation of their hard work. Everyone in the room cheered exuberantly. "Six months?" came next. "Six months? . . . Three months? . . . Two months? . . . Two months? . . ." Yet nobody stood to receive a chip. After a moment, the speaker continued: "Finally, and perhaps most important of all, 24 hours without a drink?" One woman stood, grabbed the token without making eye contact with anyone in the room, and quickly sat back in her seat, squirreling away her prized possession. She got the most rousing round of applause of all.

When the room finally settled down, the speaker asked one final question. "To prove that AA and these meetings work, can we get a show of hands from those who have been clean and sober for a year or more?" Over half of the attendees raised a hand, and more sounds of applause spread through the room.

AA Can Be a Resource for PAs

At this point I had my second sobering realization. Alcoholics Anonymous does indeed work for people with addictions to alcohol and other substances of abuse, and the phone number for the nearest AA support group is a tool that PAs should consider as important as our ophthalmoscope or stethoscope. Local AA contact numbers should be a part of the vigilant clinician's repertoire, as it is our duty to find every possible resource and offer it to those in need.

As I think back on this experience, what really stands out is how accepting the people at this meeting were of each other. It is almost tragically beautiful that without hesitation, young embraced old, black embraced white, straight embraced gay, and all the categories and differences that segregate people in the "real world" melted away in that dirty, smelly basement. These strangers who shared this disease called alcoholism, who shared this awful experience, who shared this addiction and the pain that always accompanies it, seemed no longer to see race, creed, or color when looking at their fellow addicts. The outer shell that usually defines a person was stripped away, leaving a simple common core of someone battling to stay sober, one day at a time. These people were not looking for miracles. They were not looking to take giants leaps. They were simply looking to live life on life's terms while resisting the urge to escape into the bottom of a bottle.

Diary of My First Dry Week

Joe Stone

Facing a drunk-driving charge, Joe Stone is forced to address his alcoholism. In the following selection, Stone provides commentary on the initial pain of withdrawal and detoxification, including sleeplessness, sweating, and shaking. He records the everyday struggles of sobriety, documenting his thoughts and actions throughout his first week without alcohol. An avid soccer fan, Stone passes the week watching the World Cup tournament on television, an activity he finds particularly difficult to do without a drink. At the time he wrote the diary, Stone, who lives in London, had been sober for twelve days.

Starting to Quit Slowly

Saturday

Sitting at kitchen table opposite wife. Two cans of Pils in a blue bag between us. My final drinks, in theory, before indefinite abstention. Think of John Lennon asking Yoko Ono to tie him to a chair for three days so he could kick his heroin habit.

Wife asks if I'm going to drink them. I can hardly be bothered. Might as well be mineral water. Feel like condemned man, fearful of the dawn.

World Cup highlights flicker on the television. Germany are drawing with Paraguay. With teutonic efficiency they will score in the 88th minute. Watched the England game in the pub. Drank. Wasn't supposed to. Those two cans were my ration for today. You reduce gradually over a week. Dangerous to stop abruptly.

She asks me again. I tell her about Lennon and Yoko. She says she's going away for a week. And how would I go to the toilet? I hadn't thought of that. A very practical woman.

I open a can of Pils. A reflective sip. When the authorities used to execute people at Tyburn they used to bring them on carts down Oxford Street, where they would let them stop and have one last drink. And all because they'd nicked a loaf of bread.

Pundits pontificate. My wife asks why I'm watching their analysis with the sound turned off. It seems obvious to me. I finish the can and open the second. Throw the empty at the bin. It rolls across the floor. Some things never change. Take me to Tyburn. String me up and whip the horses.

Unable to Sleep

Sunday, early hours

Restless already. Sweating and fidgeting. Trying to get comfortable, trying to find sleep. What time the dawn? About four. The birds are starting already.

Only one thing could get me to sleep. I look across at the wife. No chance.

Old songs come into my head. And remain there. Who controls the cerebral jukebox? Not I, certainly. "Tie a Yellow Ribbon"? "Billy Don't be a Hero"? Why? I think of everything that I am manifestly unable to remember—birthdays, phone numbers, anniversaries, names, yet my mind has carefully filed the lyrics to 30-year old songs. It gets worse. "The Young Ones," darling we're the Young Ones.

Sunday, 6am

Sun is streaming in through a gap in the curtains. Pull duvet over head and sweat even more. Examine hands. Slightly tremulous. The sheets are damp and tangled. Close my eyes. Try to relax each part of my body in turn. You start with your toes, then your ankles. I give up at the calves. It would be time to get up by the time you got to sleep like that.

You all right, son, asks a concerned voice. It's the Demon within.

Don't worry. We'll sort something out.

It's good to have people you can rely on.

Sweating and Shaking

Sunday, 8am

Wife inquires about health. Put on brave face. She tells me I'm sweating. I tell her I know. Hands, she says. Like being back at primary school in the queue for dinner. She says they are shaking. I tell her I know. She says the sheets need washing. I say it will get worse before it gets better.

There's a bottle of mineral water by the bed. I drink most of it. She brings me a cup of camomile tea. Drink it two-handed. And spill it. She suggests rubber mattress cover. A very practical woman.

Sunday, 10am

Wife has gone to church. Perhaps that's what I need. Faith. Forgive me Lord, for I have sinned. And by the way, where's the altar wine?

She's opened the curtains. I can't be bothered to close them. Pull covers over head. Toss and turn, front and back, left side, right side. Should get up. Senegal against Sweden. Go to toilet. Urine dark and acrid. Back to bed. Sweating heavily.

The Temptation to Drink

Sunday, noon

Get up to watch the Ireland game. Take a shower. Shave with caution. Make tea and toast. David O'Leary talks sensibly before the game.

Game starts; toast uneaten. Spain the better side but Ireland matching them with commitment and organisation. A good game, this; in different circumstances I would enjoy it.

Exactly, says the Demon, suggesting a trip to the off licence. I thank him for his kind suggestion but demur. He says he's only thinking of me, doesn't like to see me like this.

At the off licence I purchase 20 cigarettes and two bottles of mineral water. Proprietor looks puzzled. It is as if the Pope has come in and bought a large packet of Durex Gossamer [a brand of condoms].

On return wife surveys purchases anxiously. Wonder if she's going to body search me. She holds up the cigarettes and points to the garden. Ireland are losing. On garden bench I smoke first cigarette for years. Makes me dizzy. Ireland are going home.

Sunday, 5pm

The wife leaves. Won't see her until next weekend. Read *News of the World*. Little inspiration there. It's just me and the Demon and he is deeply concerned about my welfare.

Don't like to see you like this, he says. Lost your *joie de vivre*, mate. Look at you. Sweating and shaking. Why don't you go out and get a couple of cans? Nobody will know. Get you back on your feet. You can give it up tomorrow. . . .

Another Sleepless Night

Run a hot bath. Emerge an hour later, weak and nauseous. Go to bed at seven. Lie awake as I will all night. Hot sweats, cold sweats. Begin to have minor convulsions. Nothing serious, little more than sudden involuntary twitching of arms and legs. Wonder if they will continue at work on Monday. Visions of dropping colleagues with inadvertent left hooks.

Check the clock next to the bed every few minutes. The Demon respectfully reminds me that the off licence will close earlier today as it is Sunday. I thank him for his courtesy but remind him of the necessity of my present course of action.

My solicitor has informed me that I should hopefully avoid a custodial sentence on the drink-driving charge that I currently face. If, however, I am caught committing similar offences in the meantime or subsequently then there will be little that she or anyone else in the profession will be able to do for me. In that event I will be held at a police station until I go before a magistrate, who will deny bail and remand me in custody until trial, possibly months away. And it won't be Hull Open prison, discussing the finer points of literary endeavour with Lord Archer, but in Brixton or the Scrubs, banged up four to a cell, 23 hours a day.

So thank you, Demon, but I'll take a sleepless night or two, the sweats and the shakes and I'll dance with St Vitus [patron saint of dancers].

Midnight

First 24 hours over. Calories 0. Alcohol units 0. Cigarettes 5. Eat my shorts, Bridget Jones.

Monday, 3am

Cold bath. Raid medicine cabinet. Old antibiotics, aspirin, paracetemol. Nothing of any use here. A packet of St John's wort. Banned in a lot of countries. Must be something to it. I take three tablets.

Drive to work. Weather reports threaten 80 degrees F in Central London. I'll have an excuse to be sweating heavily.

Monday, 3pm

Brazil have beaten Belgium. Will meet England on Friday. Nation begins to slide helplessly into jingoistic overload. This will be the real final, howl the media, which to me seems a bit disrespectful to the other teams involved.

Arrive home from work; open letters. Council tax is overdue, threat of legal action, costs and so forth. An invitation for a platinum credit card. Another summons. This one for a jumped light. I can plead guilty by post. There is a space in which I must fill in any mitigating circumstances. I can imagine the kind of nonsense people fill this space with; an open invitation to tell a few falsehoods. Perhaps honesty is the best approach. Sir, in mitigation I would like to inform the court that I find driving in this modern-day Babylon somewhat enervating. However, if I refrain from stopping at red lights my journey time is much reduced and I arrive at my destination in a far better frame of mind.

Hallucinations

Monday, 8pm

Mild optimism. Heading for the 48-hour mark. Thinking it's all over. Unfortunately it's not 1966 and it's certainly not all over.

Watch EastEnders. There's always someone worse off than you are. Supportive phone call from wife. Long bath. Retire to less than fragrant bed. Sleep comes quickly but with it nightmares accompanied by distant, indecipherable voices. Awake, I can still hear the voices, which seem to be coming from the adjacent house where an elderly neighbour lives alone. The bottle of mineral water by the bed is empty.

Go downstairs in late evening light. Switch kitchen light on and realise that the Demon has brought in the heavy artillery. The whole room is in motion. Walls palpitate, the floor moves, bars of light criss-cross the room and mosquito like insects fill the air. Everything in my peripheral vision is moving, shaking and trembling.

I sit down heavily, Indiana Jones in the Kitchen of Doom. I know it's not real and I'm certainly not going to try to swat any of those mosquitoes. Begin to wonder whether I should seek medical help. If this continues I will have little option. I switch off the light; the kitchen calms. Hope this is the Demon's last throw of the dice. Watch television and drink tea until dawn.

Beginning to Improve

Tuesday/Wednesday/Thursday

Feel better by the hour. Begin to sleep properly. Sweats cease. Hands steady. Digestive system starts to function appropriately.

Mood sombre, in contrast to the rest of the nation, which has been convinced by the media that England will win the World Cup.

Friday, 8am

As Michael Owen scores against a manifestly superior Brazil I begin to doubt my sanity far more than I had in a palpitating kitchen full of hallucogenic mosquitoes. I hardly watch the action, staring at the scoreline in the top left-hand corner of the screen.

England 1 Brazil 0.

After watching every competitive England fixture for more than 30 years, I find this hard to take on board. It's brief, of course; a sense of reality returns in the second half with David Seaman tangled in the side-netting, that look of heartbreaking incomprehension on his face.

Friday, 10am

I encounter an acquaintance on his way to the bookmakers. Forget the World Cup, he urges. It's Euro 2004 now. A young side, gained a lot of experience in the last three weeks, they know all about big tournaments now, they'll be coming into their prime in two years' time . . . think what price you'll get on them now. . . .

Well, there's nothing wrong with optimism, is there?

Organizations to Contact

The editors have compiled the following list of organizations concerned with the issues debated in this book. The descriptions are derived from materials provided by the organizations. All have publications or information available for interested readers. The list was compiled on the date of publication of the present volume; the information provided here may change. Be aware that many organizations take several weeks or longer to respond to inquiries, so allow as much time as possible.

Adult Children of Alcoholics
World Services Org., Inc. (ACoA)
P.O. Box 3216, Torrance, CA   90510-3216
(310) 534-1815
e-mail: info@adultchildren.org
Web site: www.adultchildren.org

Adult Children of Alcoholics World Services Org., Inc. is a 12-step recovery program for individuals who were raised in alcoholic or otherwise dysfunctional households. Newsletters and literature are available. The organization was founded in 1977 and holds meetings internationally. The group focuses on the effects of childhood experiences on adult life.

Alateen and Al-Anon
1600 Corporate Landing Parkway
Virginia Beach, VA   23454-5617
(757) 563-1600 • Fax: (757) 536-1655
e-mail: wso@al-anon.alateen.org
Web site: www.al-anon.alateen.org

Alateen was founded in 1957 and is a fellowship of young people whose lives have affected by someone else's drinking. Alateen meetings are routinely sponsored by an adult member of Al-Anon. Al-Anon, founded in 1951, is a fellowship of men, women, and children whose lives have been affected by the drinking of a family member or friend. Meetings provide the opportunity for personal growth and recovery through member support. Both Alateen and Al-Anon are based on the 12 steps of Alcoholics Anonymous and are located internationally. These programs encourage members to help themselves before they try to help others.

Alcoholics Anonymous World Services, Inc. (AA)

P.O. Box 459, New York, NY   10163
(212) 870-3400 • Fax: (212) 870-3003
Web site: www.alcoholics-anonymous.org

Alcoholics Anonymous is a 12-step fellowship of women and men who have found a solution to their drinking problems. The only requirement for membership is a desire to stop drinking. Through sharing their experience, strength, and hope, members stay sober and try to help others stay sober. Alcoholics Anonymous World Services, Inc. (AA) is supported by voluntary contributions of its members and groups and does not accept assistance from outside funding sources. This organization is based on anonymity and emphasizes the group over the individual. AA was founded in 1935 and is an international organization.

American Council for Drug Education (ACDE)

164 West 74th Street, New York, NY   10023
(800) 488-DRUG
e-mail: acde@phoenixhouse.org
Web site: www.acde.org

The American Council for Drug Education is a substance abuse prevention and education agency that develops programs and materials based on the most current scientific research on drug use and its impact on society. ACDE has an exciting range of educational programs and services designed to engage teens, address the needs of parents, and provide employers, educators, health professionals, policy makers, and the media with authoritative information on substance abuse issues.

Dual Recovery Anonymous (DRA)

P.O. Box 8107, Prairie Village, KS   66208
(877) 833-2332
Web site: www.draonline.org

Dual Recovery Anonymous is a self-help program for people suffering from an addiction as well as a mental illness, both considered to be "No-Fault Illnesses." Based on the principles of the 12 steps of AA, Dual Recovery Anonymous was founded in 1989 and has chapters internationally.

Families Anonymous (FA)

P.O. Box 3475, Culver City, CA   90231-3475
(800) 736-9805 • fax: (310) 815-9682
e-mail: famanon@familiesanonymous.org
Web site: www.familiesanonymous.org

Families Anonymous, founded in 1971, is a 12-step fellowship for relatives and friends of people with addictions or behavioral problems. Members focus on their own serenity in spite of the chaos others create in their lives. Extensive literature and a bi-monthly newsletter are available.

Moderation Management (MM)

22 West 27th Street, New York, NY   10001
(212) 871-0974
e-mail: mm@moderation.org
Web site: www.moderation.org

Moderation Management was founded in 1993 as an alternative to abstinence-based 12-step programs. This behavioral change program is designed for people who are concerned about their drinking and want to make lifestyle changes. It is a support group for those who do not feel they have an addiction but want to maintain their drinking at a socially acceptable level.

Mothers Against Drunk Driving (MADD)

511 E. John Carpenter Freeway, Suite 700, Irving, TX   75062

(214) 744-6233 • Fax: (972) 869-2206

Web site: www.madd.org

Since its founding in 1980, MADD has grown to be the largest crime victim organization in the world. MADD's goal is to reduce fatalities caused by drunk or impaired driving. Campaigns such as "Tie One On for Safety" and "Designate a Driver" have encouraged awareness about the dangers of drunk driving and safe alternatives.

National Center on Addiction and Substance Abuse at Columbia University (CASA)

633 Third Ave., New York, NY   10017

(212) 841-5200

Web site: www.casacolumbia.org

The National Center on Addiction and Substance Abuse was founded in 1992 by former U.S. Secretary of Health, Education, and Welfare Joseph A. Califano Jr. CASA aims to increase awareness of the economic and social costs of substance abuse and its impact on people's lives. It also strives to eradicate the stigma of substance abuse and replace shame and despair with hope.

National Council on Alcoholism and Drug Dependence

22 Cortlandt Street, Suite 801, New York, NY   10007

(212) 269-7797 • Fax: (212) 269-7510

e-mail: national@ncadd.org

Web site: www.ncadd.org

The National Council on Alcoholism and Drug Dependence was founded in 1944 to provide education, information, help, and hope to the public. The organization advocates for prevention, intervention, and treatment through a nationwide network of affiliates. The mission is to fight the stigma of alcohol and drug addiction and to raise awareness that such addictions are preventable and treatable.

National Institute on Alcohol Abuse and Alcoholism (NIAAA)
5635 Fishers Lane, Bethesda, MD   20892
(301) 443-3860
e-mail: niaaaweb-r@exchange.nih.gov
Web site: www.niaaa.nih.gov

The mission of the National Institute on Alcohol Abuse and Alcoholism is to conduct scientific research to determine the biological effects of alcohol consumption. It was founded in 1970 to combat the major public health problems of alcohol abuse and alcoholism. NIAAA provides helpful information to public health officials in hopes of preventing alcohol abuse and improving necessary treatment.

National Organization on Fetal Alcohol Syndrome (NOFAS)
900 17th St. NW, Suite 910, Washington, DC   20006
(202) 785-4585 • Fax: (202) 466-6456
Web site: www.nofas.org

The National Organization on Fetal Alcohol Syndrome works to increase public awareness about fetal alcohol syndrome (FAS) and represents the interests of persons with FAS and their caregivers. NOFAS is a politically active group and has helped legitimize FAS as a developmental disability. NOFAS endeavors to reduce the stigma and improve the quality of life for affected individuals and families. Although there is no cure or treatment for FAS, both prevention and support services are available.

Secular Organizations for Sobriety (Save Ourselves)
4773 Hollywood Boulevard, Hollywood, CA   90027
(323) 666-4295 • Fax: (323) 666-4271
e-mail: sos@cfiwest.org
Web site: www.cfiwest.org/sos

Secular Organizations for Sobriety was founded in 1986 and has become, an increasingly popular alternative to spiritually based 12-step programs. Sobriety is considered an individual responsibility and members are expected to maintain sobriety without reliance on a "higher power." Newsletters, online chats, and e-groups are available.

Students Against Destructive Decisions (SADD)
255 Main Street, Marlborough, MA   01752
(877) SADD-INC • Fax: (508) 481-5759
e-mail: info@sadd.org
Web site: www.sadd.org

Originally named Students Against Drunk Driving, SADD was founded in 1981 and has become the nation's largest peer-to-peer youth education and prevention organization with thousands of chapters in middle schools, high schools, and colleges. The goal of SADD is to provide students with the best prevention and intervention tools possible for dealing with the issues of underage drinking, drug use, impaired driving, and other destructive decisions.

Substance Abuse and Mental Health Services Administration (SAMHSA)
1 Choke Cherry Road, Rockville, MD   20850
(240) 276-2000 • Fax: (240) 276-2010
Web site: www.samhsa.gov

The Substance Abuse and Mental Health Services Administration has focused its mission on building resilience and facilitating recovery for people with, or at risk for, mental or substance use disorders. SAMHSA ensures that prevention and treatment programs are effective and available to all who are in need. The organization acknowledges the correlation between substance abuse and mental illness and provides current information on this topic.

For Further Reading

Books

Alcoholics Anonymous. New York: Alcoholics Anonymous World Services, 2001.

Drew Barrymore, *Little Girl Lost.* New York: Pocket Books, 1991.

Chris Beckman, *Clean: A New Generation in Recovery Speaks Out.* Center City, MN: Hazelden, 2005.

Claudia Black, *Children of Alcoholics: It Will Never Happen to Me.* New York: Random House, 1981.

Jack Canfield and Mark Victor Hansen, *Chicken Soup for the Teenage Soul: The Real Deal Challenges: Stories About Disses, Losses, Messes, Stresses, and More.* Deerfield Beach, FL: Health Communications, Inc., 2006.

Jane Claypool, *Alcohol and You.* New York: Franklin Watts, 1981.

Sharon W. Cruse, *Another Chance: Hope and Health for the Alcoholic Family.* Palo Alto, CA: Science and Behavior Books, Inc., 1989.

Paul Dolmetsch, ed., *Teens Talk about Alcohol and Alcoholism.* Garden City, NY: Doubleday, 1987.

George B. Eager, *Peer Pressure.* Valdosta, GA: Mailbox Clubs Books, 1993.

James Frey, *A Million Little Pieces.* New York: Anchor Books, 2004.

Donald W. Goodwin, *Alcoholism: The Facts.* New York: Oxford University Press, Inc., 2000.

Victoria C. G. Greenleaf, *Fighting the Good Fight: One Family's Struggle against Adolescent Alcoholism*. Fort Bragg, CA: Cypress House, 2002.

Pete Hamill, *A Drinking Life: A Memoir*. New York: Deidre Enterprises, Inc., 1994.

Suzanne E. Harrill, *Empowering Teens to Build Self-Esteem*. Houston: Innerworks Publishing, 1996.

Margaret O. Hyde, *Alcohol 101: An Overview for Teens*. Brookfield, CT: Twenty-First Century Books, 1999.

Guy Kettelhack, *Firt Year Sobriety: When All That Changes Is Everything*. Center City, MN: Hazelden, 1992.

Alan Lang, *Alcohol: Teenage Drinking*. New York: Chelsea House, 1992.

Maryann Lenzi, *Portraits of My Life: Looking Back as an Adult Child of Alcoholism*. North Wales, PA: Beaver Publications, Inc., 2001.

Shelly Marshall, *Young, Sober, and Free*. Center City, MN: Hazelden, 2003.

Joyce Meyer, *Teenagers Are People Too!* New York: Warner Books, Inc., 2002.

Barbara Robinette Moss, *Change Me into Zeus's Daughter: A Memoir*. New York: Scribner, 2000.

George Murphy, *Suicide in Alcoholism*. New York: Oxford University Press, Inc., 1992.

John R., *Big Book Unplugged: A Young Person's Guide to Alcoholics Anonymous*. Center City, MN: Hazelden, 2003.

Judith Seixas, *Children of Alcoholism*. New York: HarperCollins Publishers, Inc., 1985.

Becky Tirabassi and Greg Lewis, *The Life of the Party: A True Story of Teenage Alcoholism*. Grand Rapids, MI: Campus Life Books, 1990.

Stephen Tropiano, *Rebels and Chicks: A History of the Hollywood Teen Movie.* New York: Back Stage Books, 2006.

Twenty-four Hours a Day for Teens: Daily Meditations. Center City, MN: Hazelden, 2004.

Dennis Wholey, *The Courage to Change: Personal Conversation about Alcoholism with Dennis Wholey.* Boston: Houghton Mifflin Company, 1984.

Periodicals

Alcohol Health and Research World, "Adolescent Drinking," Winter 1991.

Jim Bernat, "My Boyfriend Was a Binge Drinker," *Teen Magazine*, December 1995.

David Bjerllie, "Danger in the Passenger Seat," *Time*, August 25, 2003.

Tony D. Crespi and Ronald M. Sabatelli, "Children of Alcoholics and Adolescence: Individuation, Development, and Family Systems," *Adolescence*, summer 1997.

Robert Crosnoe, "The Connection Between Academic Failure and Adolescent Drinking in Secondary School," *Sociology of Education*, vol. 79, no. 1, January 2006.

Diverse Issues in Higher Education, "Teenagers Exposed to Alcohol Ads Drink More," vol. 23, no. 1, February 23, 2006.

John Elson, "Drink Until You Finally Drop," *Time*, December 16, 1991.

Helen Fields, "It's Time for That Talk about Alcohol," *U.S. News and World Report*, March 16, 2006.

Erin Harmon as told to Mark J. Miller, "I'm an Alcoholic," *Teen People*, vol. 8, no. 5, June–July 2005.

Alex Kingsbury, "From Smashed to a Smash," *U.S. News and World Report*, March 14, 2005.

Erin Mindell, "Statistics on Teen Drinking," *Topeka Capital-Journal*, March 19, 2000.

W. Reed Moran, "Suzanne Somers Speaks for Children of Alcoholics," *USA Today*, February 26, 2001.

Newsday, "Sobering Facts on the Dangers of Alcohol," April 24, 2002.

Oakland Tribune, "Educate Teens about Dangers of Drinking," May 14, 2004.

Elizabeth Querma, "Teenagers and Alcohol," *U.S. News and World Report*, October 12, 2004.

Elizabeth Querma, "Teen Drinking," *U.S. News and World Report*, September 14, 2004.

SciTech Book News, "Alcohol Information for Teens: Health Tips about Alcohol and Alcoholism, including Facts about Underage Drinking," June 2005.

Vegetarian Times, "You Booze, You Lose," June 2005.

Jeffrey S. Wolfsberg, "The Successful Prevention of Underage Drinking and Other Drug Use: An Integrated Approach," *Independent School*, vol. 66, no. 2, winter 2007.

Internet Sources

About Alcoholism and Substance Abuse, "Alcohol, Delinquency Plagues 1/3 of U.S. Teens," April 6, 2005. www.alcoholism.about.com.

About Alcoholism and Substance Abuse, "Teen Brain Affected by Depression, Alcoholism," November 23, 2003. www.alcoholism.about.com.

American Academy of Family Physicians, "Teen Drinking: It Can Spin Your World Around," 2000. www.aafp.org.

Baptist Memorial Health Care, "Alcoholism—Causes," 1997. www.baptistonline.org.

Baptist Memorial Health Care, "Teenage Drinking," 1997. www.baptistonline.org.

Drug Rehabs, "Teens and Alcohol: The Risks." www.drug rehabs.com.

Carma Haley "Teen Thoughts on Drinking." www.teenagers today.com.

Intervention Guide, "Signs of Teen Alcoholism and/or Addiction." www.interventionguide.com.

Dixie Jordan, "The Danger Zone," 1998. www.parent teen.com.

Kiwibox.com, "Alcoholism," 2000. www.kiwibox.com.

MSN, "Recovered Celebrity Alcoholics." www.msn.handbag .com.

National Youth Violence Prevention Resource Center, "Teens and Alcohol." www.safeyouth.org.

Tatyana Parsons, "Alcoholism and Its Effect on the Family," December 14, 2003. www.allpsych.com.

RAND Corporation Health, "Teenage Alcohol Misuse," 1998. www.rand.org.

Suite 101, "Alcohol and Teens: The Link between Alcohol and Juvenile Delinquency," February 20, 2007. www.suite101.com.

Suite 101, "Too Young to Get Sober: and Other Common Myths and Misconceptions," February 7, 2007. www.suite101.com.

TeensHealth, "Alcohol." www.kidshealth.org.

Becky Tirabassi, "I Was a Teenage Alcoholic," 2005. www.briomag.com.

WebMD, "Understanding Alcohol Abuse—the Basics," 2002. www.webmd.com.

Tamar Weiss, "So What's Wrong with a Few Drinks?" www.teenagerstoday.com.

Index

A

AA. *See* Alcoholics Anonymous World Services, Inc.

Abandonment, feelings of, 73, 80, 86–87, 88, 90

Absenteeism, alcohol-related, 11

Abstinence, 12–13, 54–56
    See also Drinking, quitting

Accidents, alcohol-related, 11, 20, 82
    See also Driving under the influence

Addictions
    codependency and, 69–72
    failure to recognize, 36, 45
    in families, 13, 48–63, 127
    recovery, 110–113, 116–117, 127, 128
    See also Alcoholism; Denial; Drug abuse

Adult Children of Alcoholics World Services Org., Inc. (ACoA), 125

Advertising, 11–12

The Advocate (journal), 110

Al-Anon, 125–126

Alateen, 13, 56, 125–126

Alcohol
    abstinence from, 12–13, 54–56
    effects on teenagers, 10–11, 13, 25–27, 90
    experimenting with, 28, 110

Alcohol companies, 11

Alcohol poisoning, 25–27

Alcoholics
    behavior of, 31, 40–43, 50–51, 72, 94, 110
    functional, 54–56

personal accounts, 16–46, 118–124

Alcoholics Anonymous World Services, Inc. (AA), 12–13, 81, 100, 107, 126, 127
    open meetings, 56, 114–117
    reliance on, 111, 113

Alcoholism
    causes, 26–27, 67, 69–72, 80–82, 88–90, 110–113
    consequences, 11, 13, 29, 39, 81
    depression and, 73, 78, 82, 86–87, 113
    as disease, 80, 88–89, 105, 107, 115, 117
    mental illness and, 11, 69, 72, 130
    parents and, 48–63, 125–126
    prevention of, 12, 89, 105, 107, 128, 129, 130
    progression of, 36–46, 110–111
    recovery from, 71–72, 79, 80–82, 84, 107, 110–130
    teenage, 10–14, 16–46, 90, 125

Alienation, feelings of, 16, 50, 116

American Council for Drug Education (ACDE), 126

Amnesia, alcohol-induced, 17–22, 61

Anger, alcoholism caused by, 80

Anxieties, alcoholism caused by, 26–27, 67, 82, 111

Arrests, alcohol-related, 11

B

Behavior problems, 94, 127
    See also Alcoholics, behavior of; Mental illnesses

Emotional problems, alcoholism caused by, 10, 69–72
See also Depression
Enabling, 57–58, 63, 69–72, 84
distancing to avoid, 79, 88–89
Environmental factors, 71
Escape, alcohol as, 11, 39, 117
Estrangement. *See* Alienation, feelings of
Experimentation, 28, 110

F

Families
alcoholism in, 11, 13, 29, 48–63, 125, 127
dysfunctional, 70–72, 125
support from, 110, 112–113
See also Children; Parents; Teenagers
Families Anonymous (FA), 127
Fetal alcohol syndrome (FAS), 129
Flunitrazepam (drug), 25
Frey, Colleen and Marian (children of alcoholic), 77–78, 80–81, 87–88, 91–92, 95, 99
Frey, Raymond (partner of alcoholic), 80, 81, 86, 87
Friends
alcoholic, 13, 33–35, 65–72, 125–126, 127
drinking with, 16, 19–20, 39, 40
support from, 12, 51, 53, 55, 110, 112–113
See also Peer pressure
Functional alcoholics, 54–56

G

Genetic factors, 50–51, 56, 69, 71–72, 90, 110
Group therapy, 36, 38–39
Guilt, feelings of, 24, 31, 33, 39, 51

H

Hallucinations, as withdrawal symptom, 122–123
Hangovers, 30, 36
Help, asking for, 38–39, 52–53, 81
See also Self-help programs; Support groups
High school students, alcohol consumption, 10, 16–36
Homelessness, 88, 89
Honesty, as recovery aid, 81, 113
Hope, 12–13, 128
Humility, as recovery aid, 70

I

Illnesses, alcohol-related, 11
Interventions, 89, 105, 107, 128, 130
See also Prevention programs
Isolation, feelings of, 54, 56, 65–68, 87

J

Joy to You and Me Enterprises (Web site), 69

L

The Lawyers Assistance Program, 110, 111, 113
Lennon, John, 118
Liquid courage, alcohol as, 11
Loneliness, feelings of, 54, 56, 65–68, 87
Love, as recovery aid, 69, 70–71, 76, 87–91

M

MADD (Mothers Against Drunk Driving), 127–128
Maturity factors, 10, 13

U

Unconsciousness, alcohol-induced, 10, 26

See also Amnesia, alcohol-induced; Blackouts

V

Verbal abuse. *See* Families, dysfunctional

Volkmann, Toren (alcoholic), 36–46

Vomiting, alcohol-induced, 10, 22–24

W

Warnat, Mark, 114

Who Do You Love (Thompson), 65

Wild Blue Yonder (Thompson), 65

Wilson, Ann (sibling of alcoholic), 76, 77, 84

Withdrawal, 70, 82–84, 91–95
personal accounts, 36, 38–39, 118–124

Writers, alcohol and, 65–67

Z

Zailckas, Koren (alcoholic), 16–35